4 RENEWABLE

PowerPoint® 2007 Graphics & Animation

Made EASY

PowerPoint® 2007 Graphics & Animation

Made EASY

S. E. Slack

Michelle I. Zavala

McGraw Hill

New York Chicago San Francisco
Lisbon London Madrid Mexico City
Milan New Delhi San Juan
Seoul Singapore Sydney Toronto

The McGraw·Hill Companies

Cataloging-in-Publication Data is on file with the Library of Congress

McGraw-Hill books are available at special quantity discounts to use as premiums and sales promotions, or for use in corporate training programs. To contact a special sales representative, please visit the Contact Us page at www.mhprofessional.com.

PowerPoint® 2007 Graphics and Animation Made Easy

1234567890 DOC DOC 0198

ISBN   978-0-07-160076-7
MHID   0-07-160076-0

Sponsoring Editor	**Acquisitions Coordinator**	**Indexer**	**Series Design**
Roger Stewart	Carly Stapleton	Rebecca Plunkett	Dodie Shoemaker
Editorial Supervisor	**Technical Editor**	**Production Supervisor**	**Art Director, Cover**
Janet Walden	Jennifer Kettell	Jean Bodeaux	Jeff Weeks
Project Editor	**Copy Editor**	**Composition**	**Cover Designer**
LeeAnn Pickrell	LeeAnn Pickrell	Dodie Shoemaker	Jeff Weeks
	Proofreader		
	Susie Elkind		

About the Authors

S. E. Slack is a lifestyle and technology writer and author with more than 17 years of experience in business writing. Since the early 1990s, she has been a fan of PowerPoint. She has used it extensively in both professional and personal settings and has trained others on how to use its various features. As a communications professional, she is skilled at using graphics and animations to support a point without detracting from the message at hand. She uses PowerPoint 2007 regularly and has created more than 50 online training clips on the topic.

As a writer with more than 25 years of experience, **Michelle I. Zavala** is proficient in creating PowerPoint presentations in the business environment. She enjoys telling client stories in dynamic, interesting ways and credits PowerPoint 2007 for adding more punch to even the simplest presentations. She has developed PowerPoint presentations for a variety of audiences including customers, corporate executives, and stakeholders.

Contents at a Glance

Acknowledgments

There are many people behind the scenes who work tirelessly to bring a book from concept to the bookshelf. First and foremost, I'd like to thank Roger Stewart at McGraw-Hill for giving me the opportunity to share my experiences with other PowerPoint users through this book. Without his vision and guidance, this book would never have been written.

Carly Stapleton at McGraw-Hill is always a joy to work with; many thanks to her for gently prodding me along! Thanks to Jennifer Kettell for her technical review. From a production standpoint, kudos go to LeeAnn Pickrell for all the work she did to make me look and sound good in print. LeeAnn is a copy editor extraordinaire with the patience to match. And a big thank you to everyone behind the scenes who helped with graphics and other editing details. Your expertise is greatly appreciated.

I cannot write these acknowledgments without mentioning Neil Salkind and Studio B. Neil, you are a continuing inspiration to me, and I thank you from the bottom of my heart for all you do for me. You are heads and shoulders above all other agents; you have my undying trust and loyalty. Studio B, too, is forever in my heart. I couldn't do what I do without each and every one of you at Studio B who ensure I can continue to do what I love best.

Finally, thanks to Greg and Alia for lighting up my life with daily animation.

—S. E. Slack

Sally, thank you for believing in me. Your expertise, guidance, and humor made this a fun, rewarding experience.

My thanks to Roger Stewart at McGraw-Hill for taking a chance on me and to Carly Stapleton at McGraw-Hill for coordinating the content seamlessly. Thank you also to Lee Ann Pickrell for paying attention to the details while making my words "gel" consistently across the pages and to Jennifer Kettell for dealing with the particulars involved in the technical edit.

Many thanks to the behind-the-scenes folks who made the hard work look easy on the graphics and editing side of things. And thank yous would not be complete without a shout-out to Neil Salkind, agent extraordinaire, and to Studio B.

Last but not least, a heartfelt thank you to my family for bringing love and laughter into my life, and to God for loving me as only He can and blessing me as only He does.

—Michelle I. Zavala

Introduction

You know the basics of PowerPoint 2007; now it's time to create imaginative graphics and animations that capture your audience's attention. As long-time users of PowerPoint, we've designed this book to help you understand and use graphics and animations as easily as possible so you, too, can create professional, polished presentations with ease. In this book, you'll discover how to create and effectively apply SmartArt, WordArt, charts, tables, shapes, and custom animations. You'll also learn how to work with photos, clip art, movies, and sounds to give your presentations a distinctive and professional look.

Along with information on designing general layouts using PowerPoint 2007's built-in features, this book also explains each of PowerPoint's ten basic graphic and animation types. The final part of the book will discuss how to use PowerPoint graphics with Excel and Word, as well as how to rehearse your presentation to verify your graphics and animations are working perfectly.

Throughout the book, you'll find

- Step-by-step instructions and practical advice

- One-of-a-kind tips for creating and applying PowerPoint 2007 graphics and animations

- Screen captures, photos, and art wherever it is needed so you can visualize and understand the topic under discussion

- Briefings, which are short, nontechnical backgrounders on relevant people, companies, and technologies or topics of interest

- Memos, which are marginal notes, tips, and reminders that offer useful advice or warn you about potential hazards

- The Easy Way, handy tips that provide information about the best way to use features so you can accomplish tasks more easily

As you read each chapter, keep an eye out for these helpful elements.

Creating Slide Layouts That Pop

PowerPoint 2007 is a terrific tool to help others understand and remember condensed information in a memorable way. Typically, PowerPoint presentations consist of *slides* that rely on a combination of *words* (text) and *images* (graphics and/or animations) to drive home a point. The way you combine these elements creates the *design* (*layout*) of the slide. Layouts are crucial to making a slide understandable and unforgettable.

By combining text and visual objects on a slide, you can reach nearly every member of an audience with your message. The trick to using PowerPoint graphics and animations effectively, however, is to place the objects on the slide in a pleasing manner. Too many objects on a single slide, for example, and the audience can lose the entire point you're attempting to make. But a single object used properly will successfully capture an audience's attention and drive home the information.

In this chapter, we'll take a look at some basic design concepts to help you lay out your text, graphics, and animations as effectively as possible. Understanding typography, design principles, and the basics of designing a layout set the foundation for creating powerful presentations using PowerPoint 2007.

Understanding Typography

In its most basic form, *typography* is the art and technique of type design, characters, and arrangement. When we say *type,* we mean the *text* on your slide—*type* is how text on a page has been referred to for hundreds of years. The text should be set on the page to produce a readable, articulate, and visually satisfying whole object that makes it easy for readers to find what they want to read on a page.

In the old days, setting typography was a very specialized occupation. Creating the text, designing the pages, and setting them for printing took special skill and knowledge. Text wasn't just thrown onto a page; it was carefully set to emphasize certain stories or illustrations. That emphasis was thoughtfully designed to bring readers quickly to main points on a page and then to lead them to other information on the same page. The goal, of course, was to provide a memorable story so the reader could retain the information provided—just like you do with a PowerPoint slide. Figure 1-1 shows an example of a 1949 newspaper front page set by a typographer. The arrangement and appearance of the printed matter was carefully constructed to make a lasting impression upon the reader.

See how the text (headline) is arranged to capture the reader's attention with the most important stories (at least, according to the editor) in the largest size and lesser stories in smaller sizes? And the text is arranged in columns. The layout isn't fancy, but it gets the point across that Dinwiddie's retirement and the unearthing of skeletons in a local river are the most important items for the reader to note, with blood bank and business profiles being less important. Your eye is drawn to the Dinwiddie and skeletal remains stories first and to the other stories next.

All too often, people forget that graphics and animations should be used to illustrate a point in a PowerPoint presentation. Often, that point is going to be

Figure 1-1 The front page from the 1949 *Loveland Round-up*

2

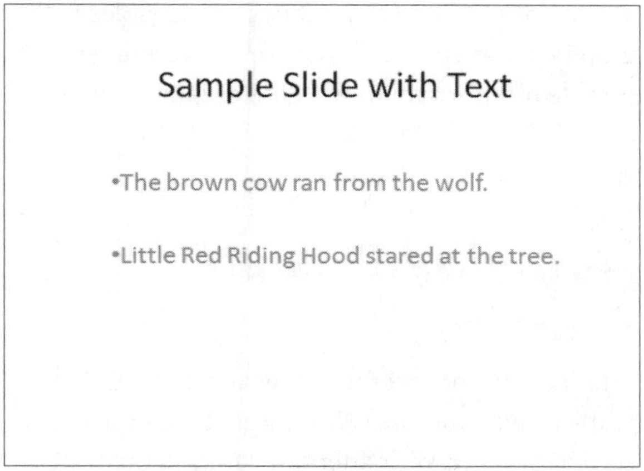

Sample Slide with Text
•The brown cow ran from the wolf.
•Little Red Riding Hood stared at the tree.

Figure 1-2 Slide with text only

presented in a text format. So understanding how to set up text on a slide so it is attractive and aids readers in following your messages is important. The graphics and animations you use should *support* those messages—they should never detract from them.

Figures 1-2 through 1-4 show examples of what we mean.

In Figure 1-2, you can see the primary points that the author needs to make. Even if nothing else is retained, the audience should remember these key points.

In Figure 1-3, graphics have been added. But look closely—how easy is it to find the primary points? It's not easy, is it? That's because the graphics completely overwhelm the text.

In Figure 1-4, however, the graphic(s) are more restrained. As a result, the primary points are easy to spot. The graphics support the text instead of overwhelm it.

You can read entire books that explain the concept of typography and how you can use it in today's digital world. If you're interested in becoming an expert in graphic design, these books might interest you. But for the purposes of this book, just keep the concept of typography in mind. Be sure the text clearly states your main points and is simple for readers to follow and understand. *Then* include graphics and

Sample Slide with text and lots of graphics
•The brown cow ran from the wolf.
•Little Red Riding Hood stared at the tree.

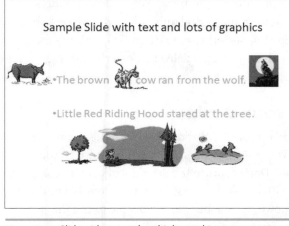

Figure 1-3 Slide with text and multiple graphics

Link *Thinking with Type: A Critical Guide for Designers, Writers, Editors, & Students (Design Briefs)*, by Ellen Lupton, Princeton Architectural Press, 2004.

Sample Slide with text with simple graphics

•The brown cow ran from the wolf.

•Little Red Riding Hood stared at the tree.

Figure 1-4 Slide with text and simple, supporting graphics

animations. If you start out designing slides with graphics first and text last, your slides will be a jumble of information with the emphasis on a graphic instead of on the message that you want your audience to retain.

Applying Design Principles

Think about the last magazine ad you read that really caught your eye. What was it about that ad that grabbed your attention? Maybe the text colors really appealed to you, or perhaps the image supporting the text was so stunning that you couldn't take your eyes off it. Or maybe it was the way that the entire ad was put together . . . the ad simply drew you in, and you couldn't not read it. Whatever it was, the underlying element was a terrific design that captured your attention long enough to deliver the advertiser's message.

As you're working with graphics and animations in PowerPoint 2007, you'll want to keep some basic design principles in mind. We've already addressed the concept of ensuring that your graphics and animations don't overwhelm any text on the slide; the following design principles can help solidify the entire blueprint of the slide to help you truly deliver a powerful message to a viewer's brain.

Create a Use for Your Design

When you sit down to design a PowerPoint slide, think carefully about how the design will be used. Do you want it to illustrate a point? Solve a problem for the reader? Inspire action? Don't confuse the design work you're doing with art—art is personal expression. Design, however, is about getting people to use the information you're providing.

Ask yourself: Does this work well? Does this

Link *Typography Workbook: A Real-World Guide to Using Type in Graphic Design*, by Timothy Samara, Rockport Publishers, 2006.

design do what I want it to do? If the answer is, "Well, it sure looks good!" then the design is probably not a good one for a PowerPoint presentation. If the answer, on the other hand, is something like, "It inspires me to want to take action" (or meets another goal you have in mind), then your design works well.

Keep the Design Invisible

When a design works well, the work you put into it is pretty much invisible to the viewer. Take the automobile, for example. It doesn't matter which auto you think of; they are all extremely sophisticated and intricately designed. Yet most people rarely consider the years of work involved in the detailed design. They simply get in and drive, expecting the auto to work without any thought on their part. The reality of the design is invisible; the final product is used successfully to solve a problem (get people from point A to point B).

If your slides are too overwrought with design concepts—if you try to cram too much onto a slide or illustrate too many points at once—your design

5

GRAPHIC DESIGN TRENDS

There is a graphic design trend afoot that arose from the work of architect Ludwig Mies van der Rohe: Less is more. Mies, as he was referred to by most, is considered a modern architectural pioneer. He worked with intense clarity and minimalism in the post World War I era, using contemporary materials such as plate glass and industrial steel to define interior spaces. His revolutionary idea was that architecture needed just a minimal structural framework alongside free-flowing open space in order to provide balance and clarity. Why clutter the architecture with lots of unnecessary details when the primary point of the structure was to connect people and activities?

In graphic design, the less-is-more concept works in much the same way. Restraint, order, balance,

harmony, and simplicity go a long way toward helping a reader recognize and retain the message you're sending. John Maeda's book, *The Laws of Simplicity* (MIT Press), is a terrific read that teaches people how to need less and get more in business, technology, design, and life.

To Maeda, simplicity and complexity will always need each other—and the more complexity there is in the world, the more something simple will stand out. The same idea can be applied to PowerPoint slides. As readers are constantly bombarded with increasingly complex items such as cell phones with 100-page instruction books, a refreshingly straightforward slide can drive home a point simply because it is so unlike the complex surroundings we live in.

will be awkward to follow, difficult to understand, and too complex for most people to keep viewing.

Think in Simple Terms

Often, the simplest design is the one that works best. Think of the wheel, for instance: a simple circle, improved upon with different types of materials for different types of requirements, but at the core, always a simple circle.

You don't always need to break down your slide designs into the simplest common denominator, but you should take a look at your design and ask, "What can I remove without losing effectiveness?"

As you design your slides, thoughtfully consider what should be kept—and what can be tossed. If you're always watching for those elements that distract from the audience experience, your designs will always be simple and easy for the audience to understand and retain.

Play with Visual Balance

If you carry a 20 pound backpack on your right shoulder for a mile, chances are you will eventually want to shift that backpack to the other shoulder. Maybe you'll want to shift the backpack so both shoulders are carrying the load instead of walking with one side of your body off-balance.

When you design a slide, visual balance is often used—elements on the slide are equally arranged so that no single portion of the slide is too heavy or too light. Sometimes, however, you can drive home a point by purposely playing with the concept of visual balance. If you place a variety of elements in the lower-right corner of a slide, for example, the viewer's eye will be drawn to that portion of the slide. Figures 1-5 through 1-7 show some examples of how you can play with balance on PowerPoint slides.

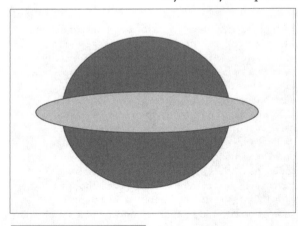

Figure 1-5 An example of horizontal balance

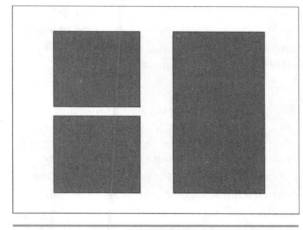

Figure 1-6   An example of vertical balance

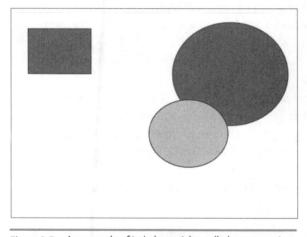

Figure 1-7   An example of imbalance (also called *asymmetry*)

The point here is to allow yourself some leeway in your design. Try not to trap yourself into using the same visual balance on every slide—your audience will be intrigued even by minor variations from slide to slide. Using the same exact visual balance on every slide can cause boredom and create wandering eyes.

Use White Space, Don't Ignore It

When you're designing layouts, any blank space on the slide is called *white space*. Don't confuse white space with any colors you might have on the slide; *white space* is the term that refers only to empty space ... not a particular color.

Although white space makes some people nervous, it's actually a good thing because it provides the reader's eye with a bit of a break as she views the slide. If you're the type of person who thinks every square inch on a slide needs to be filled, take a deep breath and remind yourself that white space is okay. Resist the urge to fill in every spot on the slide, and your readers will thank you for it. In Figure 1-8, there is white space between each line of text and plenty of white space surrounding the graphics as well. White space, by the way, isn't always colored white. It can be any color; the term is used to denote blank space

7

Link   *The Elements of Graphic Design: Space, Unity, Page Architecture, and Type,* by Alexander White, Allworth Press, 2002.

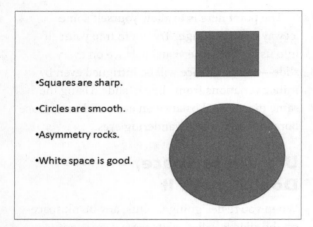

•Squares are sharp.

•Circles are smooth.

•Asymmetry rocks.

•White space is good.

Figure 1-8   Example of white space on a slide

more than any particular color. Carefully colored backgrounds coordinated with other elements can evoke different moods and enhance the whole slide from a visual perspective.

Exploring Layout Concepts

Now that you know about typography and the concept of keeping text easy-to-read, and you've learned a few basic design principles, it's time to take a look at actual layout concepts. When you're designing a slide, *layout* refers to the way that you put all the elements together. The idea, of course, is to put both text and graphic elements into a layout that is visually pleasing and simple to read.

There are as many different ways to create layouts as there are people, so don't feel as if there is a perfect way to create a slide layout. However, some layouts are nice and simple to use whereas others require lots of time and effort. To create a slide layout, you will be using placeholders for text, clip art, photos, and other objects.

As you insert each placeholder, think carefully about its location on the slide. Although you can change a placeholder's location at any time by clicking its border and dragging it to another location, if you take the time up front to think about design principles, then you'll save yourself time down the line.

Any PowerPoint slide layout can include any or all of the following elements:

- Title placeholder
- Subtitle placeholder
- Headers and footers

8

MEMO

When you change layouts, content will stay on the page, but it might be moved to accommodate the new layout.

- Body placeholder, which can be a text box, chart, picture, or graph

- Background objects

- Background fill (color or picture)

- Placeholder formatting, such as bullets

PowerPoint 2007 provides you with nine built-in layouts, as shown in Figure 1-9, but you can also create new ones from scratch or modify the built-in layouts to meet your needs. Any time you want to change a format of a particular slide, you can go to the Home tab and click Layout in the Slides group. Choose a new layout, and the slide you're working on will automatically be changed.

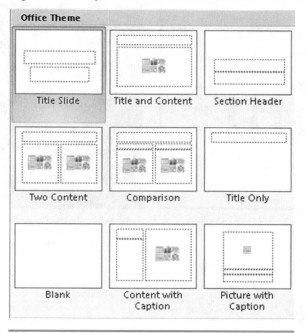

Figure 1-9   Built-in PowerPoint layouts

As you work on your layout, think about the overall subject of your presentation and any fonts, backgrounds, or PowerPoint themes you might be using. To really make a layout pop for the reader, you'll want to be sure that these types of things aren't going to compete with your placement and use of objects.

For example, in Figure 1-10, the layout is very simple and information is easy to spot. That's because the focus is on the information and supporting graphics. In Figure 1-11, however, the layout becomes much more complicated. It's the same layout used in Figure 1-10, but the addition of a PowerPoint theme makes it much harder to find the information.

So, while a layout might look terrific in one scenario, it might not work as well in another. Just keep these kinds of things in mind as you create your layouts and you'll soon find yourself catching problems before they occur.

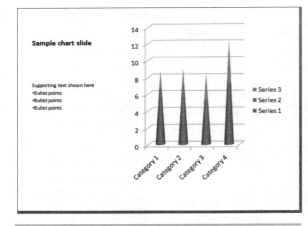

Figure 1-10   Simple layout with plain background

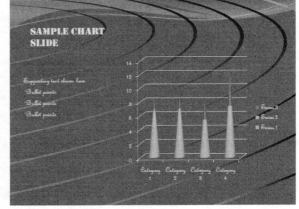

Figure 1-11   The same layout but with a PowerPoint theme and dark, wavy background applied

Link   *Graphic Design Solutions*, Third Edition, by Robin Landa, Delmar Cengage Learning, 2005

The PowerPoint Workspace

When you design a PowerPoint layout, you are working within a PowerPoint *workspace,* which has four key areas. As shown in Figure 1-12, the four areas of the PowerPoint workspace are

- **Slide pane**   Here, you can directly access and work on individual slides within a presentation. The Slide pane is used to design the actual slide layout—you'll add placeholders to it to create the design.

- **Placeholders**   These are used to insert animations, text, charts, pictures, and other objects.

- **Slides tab**   This tab is where you can see thumbnails of each slide. You can add or delete slides in this area or click and drag thumbnails to rearrange slides.

- **Notes pane**   You can use this section to enter notes about a particular slide.

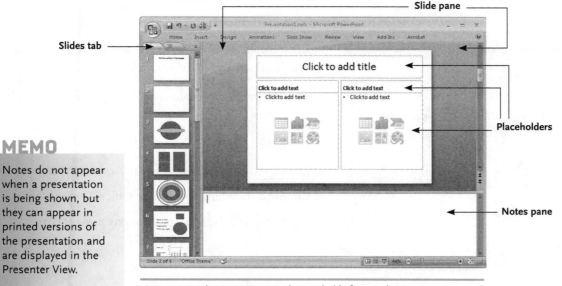

Figure 1-12   The PowerPoint workspace holds four working areas.

Adding Slides to a Presentation

As you build your presentation, you'll need to add slides to it. To do that, follow these steps:

1. Go to the Home tab.
2. Click the slide icon on the New Slide button in the Slides group.

A Title And Content Slide with title and text sections will automatically be placed into your presentation. If you simply want to duplicate a slide and change a few items on it, follow these steps:

1. Select the slide you want to duplicate on the Slides tab.
2. Click the down arrow next to the New Slide command.
3. Click Duplicate Selected Slides, and the duplicate slide will be added automatically for you.

If you want to add a completely different type of slide, follow these steps:

1. Go to the Home tab.
2. Click the down arrow next to the New Slide command.
3. Choose a slide format from the Office Theme gallery.
4. Click your selection to add it to your presentation.

MEMO

The Slide Master will only be blank if you haven't already chosen a layout or added placeholders. If you've already been working on a layout or chosen one of the PowerPoint layouts, the Slide Master will contain the elements and placeholders of that particular layout.

Working with Slide Masters and Placeholders

PowerPoint Slide Masters are the part of a slide template that stores information through the use of placeholders. When you use a Slide Master, you can make changes to a single slide (the *master*) and the changes will be applied collectively throughout your presentation. So, for example, if you want to include a company logo on every slide footer in your presentation, you can add it to the Slide Master just once, and then the logo will be shown on each slide throughout your presentation. As you add new slides, those will also include the logo. Or, you can choose to add the logo only to certain types of slides in a presentation.

Slide Masters can be easily customized. In a Slide Master, layouts are used to position placeholders (such as the logo just mentioned) in any way you want. It's a good idea to create all your Slide Masters before you start creating a presentation; slides added into a presentation are always based on the Slide Masters.

To create a Slide Master, follow these steps:

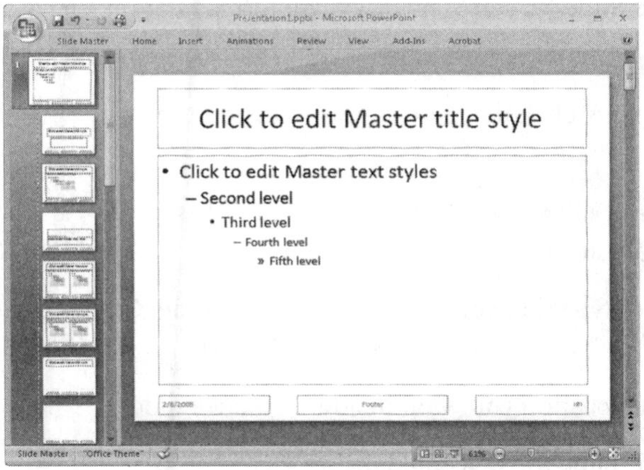

Figure 1-13   Slide Master view

1. Go to the View tab.

2. Click Slide Master in the Presentation Views group.

3. A blank Slide Master will appear in the workspace, as shown in Figure 1-13. Notice that the Slide and Outline tabs on the left have been replaced with the Thumbnail pane, which shows a master slide and multiple layout slides (also known as the *master layout*).

4. Click the Microsoft Office button.

5. Click Save As.

6. Type in a filename for the master slide layout or accept the suggested filename.

7. Click PowerPoint Template (*.potx) in the Save As Type list. Leave the default location (Templates).

8. Click Save.

9. Go to the Slide Master tab and click Close Master View in the Close group.

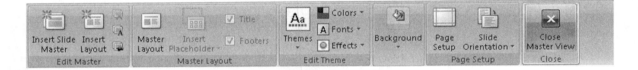

Add New Placeholders

To add text, a graphic, or other type of placeholder to a Slide Master layout, follow these steps from the Slide Master view (View tab | Presentation Views | Slide Master):

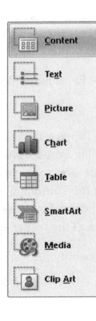

1. In the Thumbnail pane, click the slide you want to add the placeholder to.

2. Go to the Slide Master tab and click the arrow next to Insert Placeholder in the Master Layout command group.

3. Click the placeholder type that you want to add to the slide: Content, Text, Picture, Chart, Table, SmartArt, Media, or ClipArt.

4. Click the slide in the location you want to add the placeholder.

5. Drag your cursor to shape the placeholder.

6. Release the cursor to finalize placement.

Add Custom Text to a Placeholder

You might want to add custom text to single or multiple slide layouts that use text placeholders. If you do, follow these steps using the Slide Master view:

1. Click the slide that will hold the customized text.

2. In the text placeholder, type in the custom text. For example, you might want your slide to say **Add Employee Names Here** so that others using the template know where to type product information. Figure 1-14 shows an example of custom text.

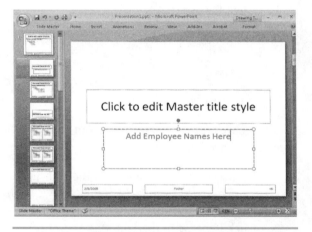

Figure 1-14   An example of how to place custom text into a placeholder

3. Go to the Slide Master tab. Click Close Master View in the Close group.

4. Go to the Home tab.

5. Click Layout in the Slides group.

6. Click the slide layout with the custom text. PowerPoint will automatically add it to your presentation.

15

MEMO

If you need to remove a placeholder, just click its border and press DELETE on your keyboard.

Want to remove an unwanted slide from a master layout? In Slide Master view, right-click the slide on the Thumbnail pane and click Delete Layout on the shortcut menu.

Rename a Slide Master or Slide Layout

If you need want to rename a Slide Master, just follow these steps:

1. Click the Slide Master to be renamed.

2. Go to the Slide Master tab.

3. Click Rename in the Edit Master group.

4. In the Rename Master dialog box, type in the new name in the Master Name box.

5. Click Rename.

Rename

If you have created a new slide layout within a Slide Master that you want to name, follow these steps:

1. In the Thumbnail pane, click the slide layout you want to rename.

2. Go to the Slide Master tab.

3. Click Rename in the Edit Master group.

4. In the Rename Layout dialog box, type in the new name in the Layout Name box.

5. Click Rename.

In this chapter, you've learned about typography, basic design principles, layout concepts, and how to work with placeholders and Master Slides in PowerPoint. In the next chapter, we'll take a look at how you can apply these concepts to create custom layouts for your presentations.

Creating Custom Layouts

The best PowerPoint presentations are the ones that carefully consider both audience and content and provide the best fit for both. Technical audiences, for example, aren't going to be confused by a presentation filled with lots of charts and minute details. More general business audiences, however, might fall asleep the very first time they see a chart. That doesn't mean you shouldn't use a chart with a business or academic audience—just that you'll need to think through a custom layout geared to help your audience follow the chart easily or keep their attention.

Every slide in your presentation tells a piece of the overall story. You can move audiences from point to point using several slides, or you can cover multiple points in a single slide. You can use color to draw attention to a specific item on the slide or place bullets in a unique manner to surprise and capture the audience's attention.

In this chapter, we'll look at how custom layouts can be used in PowerPoint presentations to grab the audience's attention from the first slide—and keep the audience focused throughout the entire presentation.

Planning Your Presentation

When you create a presentation, you'll save a lot of time and aggravation if you create an outline in PowerPoint first. It doesn't have to be exhaustive, but it should be detailed enough so you aren't constantly trying to figure out what to put on your next slide.

In Chapter 1, we explained the PowerPoint workspace. In that workspace, next to the Slides tab, is the Outline tab. Click that tab, and let's add a few slides so you can see how easily you can create an outline within PowerPoint. To begin adding slides, go to Home | Slides Group | New Slide. Then follow these steps to add a total of four slides to a blank presentation:

1. Add a Title Slide. On the title slide, type **Opening statement** in the text box labeled Click To Add Title.

OUTLINING AT A GLANCE

If you haven't done much outlining, don't let the concept overwhelm you. An *outline* is simply a method for setting up the main ideas of your presentation and associating subpoints to those main ideas. You can create outlines in many different ways; some people prefer to use full sentences, whereas others are happy to use just a few words that remind them of the basic concept they want to convey in a certain area.

Outlines are extremely helpful in organizing ideas for your presentation. You can quickly see the relationship among your different ideas; this way you know you're capturing the major and minor points required.

In general, a simple outline looks something like this:

1. Main idea
   a. Supporting concept
   b. Supporting concept
      i. Subsidiary concept
2. Main idea
   a. Supporting concept
   b. Supporting concept
   c. Subsidiary concept
      ii. Subsidiary concept

You determine how many main ideas your presentation needs to get across, as well as how many supporting concepts are required. Sometimes, you can set up a main idea and all its supporting concepts on one slide; other times, you might need multiple slides to make your points clearly and effectively. Your audience should never feel overwhelmed by too much information, however. With any outline continue to refine it as your presentation takes shape. If it looks like too much information is on one slide (particularly if you're trying to reduce text just to fit all your content on one slide), keep basic design principles in mind and don't be afraid to use multiple slides for the information.

2. Add a Comparison slide. Type **Objectives** in the text box labeled Click To Add Title. In the left comparison box, type **Current year** in the subtitle box and **What's been done** next to the bullet. In the right comparison box, type **Upcoming fiscal year** in the subtitle box and **What will be done** next to the bullet.

3. Add a blank slide. Select Insert | Text | Text Box to add a text box to the slide. Place the text box wherever you prefer on the slide. Type **Supporting data** in the text box.

4. Add a Title And Content Slide. Type **Ending statement** in the text box labeled Click To Add Title.

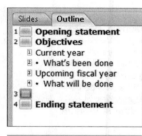

Figure 2-1   Sample outline tab showing four slides

Your outline tab should now look like the one shown in Figure 2-1.

You've just created a very simple outline in PowerPoint. Outlines can be of any length, of course, and they are extremely helpful in clarifying your thoughts and the direction of your presentation. You don't need an outline to start adding slides, graphics, and content. Without one, however, you can spend an awful lot of time trying to decide what information should go where. With an outline, you can quickly see how the presentation will flow, where you might need to add graphics and animations, and whether there are any gaps in your content plan.

Now, you've probably noticed that in Figure 2-1 no text appears next to slide 3 in the outline. Yet in step 3, you entered text for that slide. This is because you added slide 3 as a blank slide and placed a separate text box on it. When you add slides and text in that manner, the text will not appear in the outline even though the slide does. The outline only recognizes text from built-in layouts, so you need to add one to your slide by selecting the Title Only layout from the gallery.

19

THE EASY WAY

When you add a blank slide to a presentation, go to Home | Slides | Layout. Choose the Title Only layout from the gallery, and your blank slide will now have a simple built-in layout applied to it. Enter text for your outline into the headline text box provided by the Title Only layout, and then take a look at the outline tab. The previously blank slide now has text associated with it in the outline. Your slide is still essentially blank, but you can now see from the outline— and in Figure 2-2 what kind of information it should contain.

Creating Layouts to Fit Your Content

Layouts are everywhere these days. From MySpace pages to scrapbooking to PowerPoint slides, the very best layouts help you present information in a clear and direct fashion. In Chapter 1, we showed you how to access the built-in layouts offered by PowerPoint 2007. Those layouts, however, are just the tip of the iceberg. In this section, we'll show you how to create custom layouts to tell your story any way you want to.

Remember, layouts simply help you drop in the components of your slide's content—don't let them intimidate you. You don't need a graphic design background to create eye-catching, informative custom-slide layouts. All you really need is a bit of imagination and a willingness to try new ideas.

PowerPoint gives you three different ways to create custom layouts.

Slides	Outline
1	**Opening statement**
2	**Objectives**
	Current year
	• What's been done
	Upcoming fiscal year
	• What will be done
3	**Supporting data**
4	**Ending statement**

Figure 2-2 When a built-in layout is applied to a blank slide, the outline will show text from the layout's text boxes.

- You can use a blank slide and insert placeholders as needed.

- You can use a built-in slide layout and move placeholders around as desired.

- You can add a layout to a slide master in Slide Master view and then save the custom slide layout as explained in Chapter 1.

In this chapter, we'll show you some ideas for custom layouts that will help you build on the built-in layouts already provided. As we showed you in Chapter 1, any PowerPoint slide layout can include a variety of elements. Within body placeholders, there are eight

Link *Design Secrets: Layout 50 Real-Life Projects Uncovered,* by Rodney J. Moore, Rockport Publishers, 2004.

MEMO

These first two techniques are easy and handy when you simply want to make quick changes to a slide and don't plan on using the layout again in another presentation. Just create the custom slides and save the presentation as you would normally.

different types of objects you can add to create custom layouts in PowerPoint 2007:

- Shapes
- Picture
- Text
- Chart
- Table
- Media Clips
- Clip Art
- SmartArt

We'll explore the specifics of how to add and use each of these objects in later chapters; in this chapter, we'll simply show you a few ideas for custom layouts that might spark some ideas as you create your next presentation. You can customize a PowerPoint layout in literally thousands of ways, so don't *ever* be afraid to try something you haven't seen before. Here, we'll be using the simple typography and design principles explained in Chapter 1; you can always get more sophisticated and creative if you like.

First, let's look at a Title Slide. This built-in layout has two text boxes: a title text box and a subtitle text box. The text is black by default, and the text sizes and fonts are predetermined. Figure 2-3 shows an

PowerPoint Graphics and Animations Made Easy

Create professionally designed elements to make memorable presentations

Figure 2-3   A basic Title Slide in PowerPoint 2007

opening slide using only those two text boxes.

To customize this very simple slide, you could add a corporate logo or the presenter's photo. You could also move the text placeholders to other areas of the slide, apply WordArt or color, or add new placeholders to include more

PowerPoint Graphics and
Animations Made Easy

Create professionally
designed elements to make
memorable presentations

Presenter, Author

The **McGraw·Hill** Companies

Figure 2-4   A customized Title Slide in PowerPoint 2007

information about the overall presentation. Figure 2-4 shows how this very simple Title Slide could be customized to provide more details about you, your company, and the presentation topic.

In the customized example, we high-lighted the main title of the presentation in a text-colored text box, added WordArt to highlight the subtitle without overwhelming the main title, inserted the presenter's picture along with a simple text box explaining the presenter's credentials, and added the book publisher's logo to the lower-right corner of the slide.

Both slides are professional; but the addition of graphics, some WordArt, different text placement, and a bit of color makes a big difference in what the eye is drawn to on the slide. It's not fancy, but even this minor amount of customization adds pizzazz to your presentation.

Next, let's look at a Title And Content Slide, as shown in Figure 2-5. On this slide, you can add a page title along with text or one of six objects. The way the layout is built, you can't add both text *and* objects in the main portion of the slide while still retaining the main title text box across the top. But what if you want to show a picture and add supporting bullets alongside it?

You can quickly do that by resizing the text/object placeholder and then inserting a bulleted text box beside it, as shown in Figure 2-6. We used the Drawing Quick Styles gallery to add color to the bulleted text box. We then rotated both objects slightly inward toward each other. The title text placeholder remained in the same location, although we added glow to the

23

THE EASY WAY

Use the built-in Quick Style galleries to customize your slides easily. These galleries are new with PowerPoint 2007 and designed to help you instantly make big changes to plain objects. You can now add 3D, bevel, color, glow, frames, and more to your graphics and animations.

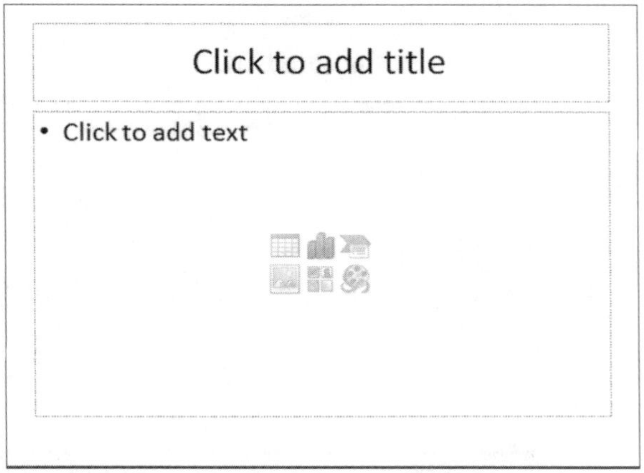

Click to add title

• Click to add text

Figure 2-5   A basic Title And Content Slide in PowerPoint 2007

text for effect. We gave the picture an instant frame using the Picture Styles gallery. All these effects and techniques will be explained throughout this book.

Here's one more idea for quick customization. Who says you have to leave a title text box at the top of a page? Sure, maybe that's where most people put titles, but remember, this is *your* slide and you can do whatever you want with it. Sometimes impact comes from placing expected elements in unexpected places. For example, in Figure 2-7, the built-in Two Content Slide

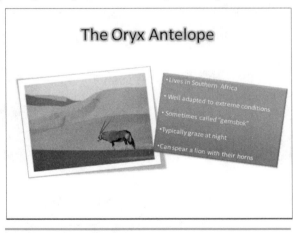

Figure 2-6   A customized Title And Content Slide in PowerPoint 2007

shows the slide title in its traditional top location with content underneath.

Now, let's take that title text box and move it to the bottom of the page, pulling the two content boxes upward. Insert some clip art, for example, to illustrate a comparison of some sort, and then type in your tagline at the

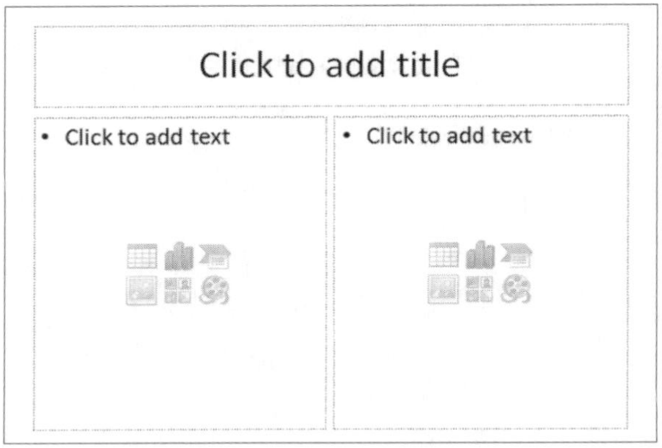

Figure 2-7   A basic Two Content Slide in PowerPoint 2007

bottom in the title text box. As you can see in Figure 2-8, you can still get the main point across without continuing a boring title text box on every single slide.

Over the next few pages, you'll see some additional layout concepts. Take a look and see if they spark any additional ideas for you. Remember, you can always add background colors and PowerPoint themes to get even more impact. In these examples, we wanted to show you how—even with plenty of white space—you can still create simple customized slides that make an impact. Later in this book, you'll see how adding animation to some of these simple customization ideas can make an even bigger impact with your audience.

Figure 2-8   A customized Two Content Slide in PowerPoint 2007

Use your own imagination when you customize a slide … for example, can a single picture tell a story? What about a shot of a stairway looking up, with the simple headline, "We're getting there" to pull the idea into focus for your audience? What about a runner

MEMO

Every slide should tell a story or lead the reader to the next slide that continues the story. As you customize your slides to meet your needs, ask yourself: Does this really make my point? Or will someone in the audience be asking, "So what?"

at a starting line to indicate that something is beginning? Or a photo of a Japanese Zen garden with the caption, "It looks simple, but it isn't."?

Generate Inspiration from Anywhere

Your layout should fit your content, not the other way around. Don't ever settle for using a layout that doesn't quite work for the information you have. PowerPoint has some good basic layouts, but your information isn't always going to work magically within those limited designs.

If you're feeling tapped out on creativity, look at a few magazines. Which ads catch your eye? If you like one in particular, copy its basic elements to your slide and then fill in with your graphics and content.

Which products in the grocery store grab your attention? Something about the packaging is making you reach for one product over another, so why not identify that key element and then try to use it somehow in your own layouts?

25

MEMO

A few more customization tips: Move text boxes into unexpected places. Layer objects in unexpected ways. Use color to impact key details. Balance objects. Don't balance objects. Turn photos or graphics in surprising directions. Visualize the information you need to share, and then create the visualization on the slide.

Some of the best graphic designers take inspiration from all kinds of things that most of us wouldn't look at twice. A tree, for instance, might spark a layout that shows how pieces of an organization fit together. A boat sailing on a choppy lake might be used to represent a rough time in history. Don't be surprised if an ad for something as mundane as women's deodorant or men's clothing inspires you. *Inspiration can come from anywhere.* Find a way to pleasantly surprise, but not startle, your audience, and you've found a custom layout worth keeping.

In this chapter, you learned about customized layouts and reviewed some customized layout concepts. In the next chapter, we'll look at several ways you can illustrate your slides with pictures.

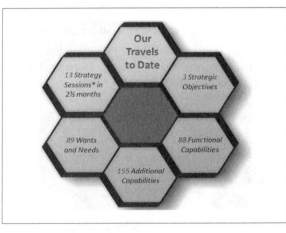

Illustrating with Pictures

Using photographs is easy in PowerPoint 2007. Once you discover the simplicity of inserting pictures and creating unique looks for each of them, you'll enjoy exploring your creativity. From setting the mood to highlighting a funny moment, PowerPoint 2007 makes the experience come alive whether you're viewing pictures for the first time or revisiting pictures that mean a lot to you. You'll learn more about creating photo albums in Chapter 4. For now, let's focus on the pictures themselves.

In this chapter, you'll learn how to adjust pictures and add special effects to create different moods and presentations. You'll also discover how to use picture styles and shapes to tell an interesting story, as well as how cropping, sizing, and framing your picture can highlight specific details of your story.

One of the fastest ways to become proficient in PowerPoint 2007 is to experiment with the many styles, special effects, and animations available. As you read through this book, remember that PowerPoint doesn't always have to be used in a business setting. Take a few minutes with each section to discover how to make PowerPoint 2007 presentations that are fun to create and will impress friends and family members.

The Picture Tools Format Tab

First, you'll need to familiarize yourself with the Picture Tools Format tab.

1. From the Home tab, click New Slide.

2. Click Blank.

3. Go to the Insert tab.

4. In the Illustrations group (see below), select Picture.

5. Select a photograph from your My Pictures folder or elsewhere on your computer.

Adjusting and Adding Effects to Pictures

MEMO

In some illustrations and figures throughout this book, you might notice a tab called Add-Ins. This nonstandard tab will only appear when you add specialized features and custom commands to PowerPoint. You can enable or disable add-ins using PowerPoint Options.

You'll be amazed at how easy it is to create effects just like the professionals. You can adjust intensity and color or add a soft glow, reflection, or beveled border to make statements that will wow your audience. And you can use these effects for PowerPoint 2007 presentations in your work life and your home life.

Don't be afraid to try new and different ways of expressing yourself. By combining adjustments and effects, you might discover the exact way you want to say something. This section addresses ways to use adjustments and effects, but remember you are limited only by your own imagination.

> You can create different folders within the My Pictures folder to help you organize your photos. As long as you categorize in a way that works for you, you'll be able to find your pictures quickly and easily.

Using the Adjust Command

Using the Adjust command group, you can change a picture to create the mood or special effects you like. The commands include:

- *Brightness* to make your photo blend or stand out more on a slide

- *Contrast* to increase or lessen the photograph's intensity

- *Recolor* to create interesting color effects that work with the slide layout

- *Compress Picture* for printing, screen viewing, or minimizing for sharing by email

Let's walk through ways to use a few of these commands to create a mood for your pictures. Insert your picture as shown in Figure 3-1.

After inserting your picture, follow these steps:

1. Select the Brightness command and change the brightness to +20%.

2. Select the Contrast command and change the contrast to +40%.

3. Select the Recolor command and select a color. The color in Figure 3-2 is Accent Color 6 Dark variation.

Figure 3-1   Insert your original picture.

Figure 3-2   The same picture with changes to brightness, contrast, and color

Figure 3-3   The same picture with a light variation

THE EASY WAY

If you're ever unhappy with your changes and want to start over again, click Reset Picture in the Adjust command group. This resets your picture to its original size, brightness, color, and contrast settings. Want to change out the photo and use a different one? Click Change Picture to go directly to the Insert Picture dialog box.

Your picture should show substantial changes, just as the one in Figure 3-2 differs from Figure 3-3.

Pictures will increase the size of your PowerPoint 2007 file, so consider using the Compress Pictures command in the Adjust group. This will save room on your hard drive and reduce download times, while maintaining picture quality. You can compress selected pictures or all of the pictures in the presentation. The compression default for PowerPoint 2007 is set to compress pictures automatically when you save the presentation and to remove the cropped area of pictures automatically. To make changes to this default setting, select Compress Pictures in the Adjust group, select Options, and click the ones you want to change.

Adding Picture Effects

You can select from six different effect categories when adding effects to your pictures. PowerPoint defaults are to never apply effects to your pictures, so if you want to do something cool to a photo, you'll have to select the option. Hover your cursor over various options in each category and watch the

PICTURE THIS...

Pictures can play an important role in presenting information in a text format. Although text is necessary for communicating with your audience, it can be overwhelming if not aesthetically designed to make it easy to digest. Bullets are one way to break up your text, but another way is to place pictures strategically on the slide.

You may have a text-only slide that, as a rule, is not interesting to look at. You could "underwhelm" your audience and their interest would wane.

Another option is to add a picture to your bulleted text. Inserting a framed oval picture on the slide increases interest.

You can invite readers in quickly by using a colorful background with the text on top. The brightness and contrast of this photo was adjusted so the text is still readable. If you're using a photo in this way, adjust brightness and contrast to make sure text is legible. Landscape pictures generally lend themselves well to this type of use. Many landscape photos have enough contrast between light and dark areas so you can arrange text for legible reading.

picture on your slide. PowerPoint 2007's Live Preview will show you exactly how the photo will look if you decide to select a particular option. Here are the effect categories and what they do:

- **Shadow** Lets you add an inner, outer, or perspective shadow to your pictures.

- **Reflection** Produces different mirror images of your photo. You can choose from nine variations.

- **Glow** Makes your pictures look extremely hip. PowerPoint has a gallery of preselected colors, but you can also click More Glow Colors at the bottom of the gallery to create your own personalized glow.

- **Soft Edges** Allows you to soften the edges of your photos. As you soften, the photo will reduce by up to 50 percent, depending on the point size option you choose.

- **Bevel** Applies different edging options to your photos. Some are soft, some have dual edging, some add angles, and so on. You can even create and add 3D options to bevel effects.

- **3-D Rotation** Lets you instantly add preset 3D options to your picture.

31

Any of these effects can bring your pictures alive at first glance. Interested in showing off a beautiful picture of the lake? Use the Reflection effect. Want to soften a picture? Add an ethereal glow to the edges. To add an effect to a picture, select the picture and then follow these steps:

1. In the Picture Styles group, select Picture Effects.

2. Select from the options to create your effect.

Figures 3-4 and 3-5 are two examples of what you can do with Picture Effects.

Figure 3-4   Bevel effect

Figure 3-5   Reflection effect

Preset gives you a way to instantly change your picture with default settings. From the Picture Tools Format tab, go to Picture Styles | Picture Effects | Preset. From the drop-down menu, you can click a preset (try Preset 11 as an example), and your picture will automatically change to reflect that setting. This is the quickest way to apply picture effects.

Using Picture Styles and Shapes

Have you ever seen a picture that stopped you in your tracks? Maybe it took your breath away or touched you deeply. Or maybe it simply made you stop for a moment and chuckle.

Although a picture itself can tell a story, the way a picture is presented can produce a dramatic effect. This section helps you better understand the difference a picture style or shape can make in telling your story through pictures. Getting your message across visually can touch your audience in a way that words, spoken or written, cannot. PowerPoint 2007 gives you all the tools you need to stylize designs that turn everyday pictures into works of art.

Using the Picture Styles Gallery

With the Picture Styles gallery, you can instantly frame your pictures using one of 23 different options, from soft or beveled edges to a thick, black frame. Let's look at a few options:

1. From the Picture Tools toolbar, click the scroll bar to the right of the Picture Styles command.

2. Hover your mouse over the different styles to see what each looks like.

3. Click to select the style you want to use.

In Figure 3-6, for example, we selected Moderate Frame, White to outline the photo and bring attention to it. In Figure 3-7, however, the choice of Compound Frame, Black outlines the photo but gives it a more classic, stately effect. In Figure 3-8, selecting Soft Edge Oval toned down the picture while still giving it a beautiful effect.

To fully use the Picture Effects command, you'll need to experiment with varying border thicknesses. Some of the effects need thicker borders to be easily visible, whereas others look more attractive with a thinner border. From the Picture Styles group, select Picture Borders. Click Weight and hover your mouse over the different line weights. Live Preview shows you the border weight. Then select the line weight you prefer.

Figure 3-6   A simple white frame highlights this picture.

Figure 3-7   A black border offers a different perspective.

34

Figure 3-8   An oval border with soft edges tones down the picture.

Link   If you need pictures for your presentation, you can find them online in the Clip Art section of Microsoft Office Online. You can also type **royalty free** in your favorite search engine and you'll find a number of sites that offer unlimited use of their photos. Some of these sites are free, whereas others charge fees. Never use a photograph in a presentation if you don't have the proper permission to use it.

35

Creating Picture Shapes

Picture Shapes offer you an easy way to make a statement with your pictures. For example, if you want to send a message to stop or halt, you can use an octagon, or stop sign, shape. Or, if you want to show progress, shape your picture as an arrow or use a shape from the Flowchart. Picture Shapes let your pictures tell the story in an interesting way, which is a subtle but fun way to grab an audience's attention.

1. From the Picture Tools Format toolbar, select the Picture Shape in the Picture Styles command group.

2. Select the shape you want to use.

The shapes shown in Figures 3-9 and 3-10 help set the mood of their respective picture. Any effects you've added to your picture will remain when you change the picture shape.

Figure 3-9   This wave shape from the Stars and Banner section in Picture Shapes flows easily across the page.

Figure 3-10   This cloud from the Basic Shapes section in Picture Shapes calls attention to a beautiful smile.

36

READY, AIM, SHOOT!

Now that you're more familiar with using pictures in PowerPoint 2007, let's take a moment to look at how you can take the best pictures possible. Although you can create numerous styles, effects, borders, and so on, to communicate your message, starting with a good picture is always your best bet for ending with an eye-catching presentation.

The first thing to understand is that spontaneous, unexpected moments can sometimes produce the best pictures. No matter how much you plan, these moments can be readily captured when you have some photography basics under your belt. Every professional photographer will tell you that being aware and knowing your camera is the best way to get those candid, impromptu moments on film or captured in your digital camera.

Every camera has its own nuances, and the way to understand these slight variations is easy: Spend time with your camera. Don't just read the instructions and wait for a good opportunity. Play! Take your camera with you everywhere for a while and start shooting. Short of dropping it, you can't break it, and if it's digital, you won't be wasting film as you practice. Learn about the different camera modes and the strength of your flash and when to use it. You'll start getting the feel for your own camera, which means that when the opportunity comes along, you'll be prepared and knowledgeable about the needed technical details.

A basic photography book will show you how to hold your camera, keeping your arms close to your sides to steady yourself and focus your pictures. You can also invest in a tripod for situations that offer plenty of time to plan and set up. So...start shooting!

Cropping, Sizing, and Framing Pictures for Maximum Effect

Resizing and framing pictures in PowerPoint 2007 means you can focus on what matters most—whether it's your child's bright smile, a business executive, or a group of friends laughing at dinner. When you edit pictures, you can add pictures styles, shapes, and borders in a variety of combinations.

The beauty of cropping, sizing, and framing pictures means you can take a so-so picture and make it stand out on the slide. Don't depend on these commands too much though. As you just learned, you're better off starting with a great picture and using these commands to enhance the photograph, rather than vice versa.

Cropping and Sizing

The basic difference between cropping and sizing is changing the content of the picture versus changing the size of the picture. *Cropping* means you remove portions of the picture such as excess space that isn't relevant. *Sizing* is simply making the picture bigger or smaller than its original size.

You can crop pictures in two ways from the Picture Tools Format toolbar: by dragging the markers or by setting the height and width in inches or percentages.

To crop by dragging the markers, follow these steps:

1.   Click Crop in the Size command group.

2. Move your cursor to one of the markers.

3. Drag the markers to resize the picture.

4. Use the 4-way arrow to move the picture on the slide.

Figure 3-11   Drag crop markers to size the picture.

Figure 3-12   An example of a cropped picture that focuses on the subject

In Figure 3-11, the crop markers can be dragged easily to the appropriate size. Figure 3-12 displays the result of a tighter, more focused picture.

To crop to size in inches, you can adjust your photo using the Size command group or the Size and Position dialog box. The Size command group is fast and easy, whereas the Size and Position dialog box gives you many more options to select from as you crop the photo. For example, you can crop the photo but also lock its aspect ratio, tell PowerPoint to select the best scale for a slide show, position the photo differently on the slide, and even add alternative text for the picture if it will be used on a website presentation.

To use the Size command group, just use the up and down arrows to make changes in the Height and Width boxes on the toolbar.

MEMO

At the bottom of the Size tab in the Size And Position dialog box, you'll be able to see the original size of your photo. Click Reset and you can instantly reset your photo to that original size.

Size and Position ? ☒

Size | Position | Alt Text

Size and rotate
Height: 4.42" ⇕   Width: 5.25" ⇕
Rotation: 0° ⇕

Scale
Height: 94% ⇕   Width: 94% ⇕
☑ Lock aspect ratio
☑ Relative to original picture size
☐ Best scale for slide show
Resolution 640 x 480 ⌄

Crop from
Left: 0" ⇕   Top: 0" ⇕
Right: 5.07" ⇕   Bottom: 3.29" ⇕

Original size
Height: 8"   Width: 10.67"
Reset

Close

To crop a photo using the Size And Position dialog box, follow these steps:

1. Click the diagonal arrow at the bottom-right corner of the Size command to display the Size And Position dialog box.

2. Adjust the height and width in the Size And Rotate section.

3. Click Close.

Link For more information on the Rule of Thirds, see *Langford's Basic Photography, Eighth Edition: The Guide for Serious Photographers*, by Michael Langford, Anna Fox, and Richard Sawdon Smith, Focal Press, 2007.

TO CROP OR NOT TO CROP

39

To crop or not to crop? When deciding whether to crop or not, take a step back and look at the picture again. What stands out most? What part of the photo do you want to highlight or focus on?

Consider the *Rule of Thirds*, which was created by Renaissance painters who wanted a picture to tell a story. The Rule of Thirds states that if you mentally divide the picture with two vertical and two horizontal lines, all evenly spaced, you will create a grid of nine sections. To create the most aesthetically pleasing composition for your picture, the object you want to highlight should be placed at the intersection(s) of the lines.

If you have a horizontal subject, it should lie on one of the horizontal lines. Vertical subjects should lie on one of the vertical lines. By not centering your subject exactly in the middle, you can crop your picture in the most interesting, inviting way.

Basically, the Rule of Thirds can take your

pictures from blah to bam! Knowing this basic rule of photography will significantly increase the impact your pictures have. Memorize this rule and start looking at photos in a gallery or in a book from your local library, and you'll see the pattern. And remember, even the most famous painters have used this rule of composition to design intriguing and interesting works of art.

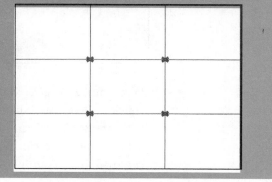

MEMO

When sizing by percentage, consider checking the Lock Aspect Ratio and Relative To Original Picture Size boxes. This will ensure that your picture maintains the ratio of height to width as you increase or decrease its size.

To size by percentage using the Size And Position dialog box, follow these steps:

1. Click on the diagonal arrow at the bottom-right corner of the Size command group.

2. In the Size And Position dialog box, select the picture size by adjusting the percentages in the Scale section.

3. Click Close.

The Size And Position dialog box also lets you rotate the picture, crop from the left, right, top, or bottom, and reset the picture to its original size. You can also position the picture on the slide from the Position tab.

1. Select the Position tab.

2. Adjust the position of picture on the slide by changing the inches from the Top-Left Corner or Center Of The Slide.

3. Click Close.

Framing Pictures

Picture borders can speak volumes when you present your pictures. A heavy border can intensify a photograph's effect, whereas a light border gives a picture an airy feel. PowerPoint 2007 gives you many options to choose from.

Below the Picture Shape command in the Picture Styles command group is Picture Border, which allows you to create a number of outlines for your pictures. You can create frames of different colors, thicknesses, and solid or patterned lines. Framing your picture in colors that complement it lets you

THE EASY WAY

You can access a few commands quickly by right-clicking on the picture. This reveals a few options that allow you to cut, copy, paste, and format the picture. The Format Picture dialog box lets you choose from a number of ways to change your picture easily. You can also find the Format Picture dialog box by clicking the diagonal arrow in the bottom-right corner of the Picture Styles group.

highlight specific details within the picture's composition. Let's add a border to a previous picture.

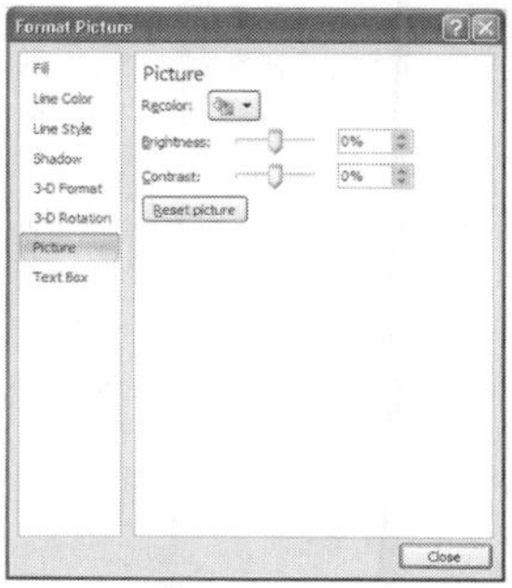

1. Select Picture Border.
2. Click Weight and select the thickness of the border.
3. Click Picture Border again.
4. Select a color for your border.

Figure 3-13 shows you how a photo looks with a 6-point, solid black border. Figure 3-14 shows the difference a light, dashed border can make at 2 ¼ points. Figure 3-15 shows how a border color can complement a picture.

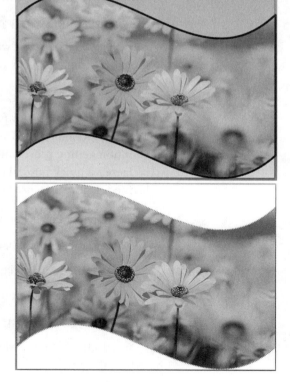

Figure 3-13 An example with a solid, black border

Figure 3-14 An example with a light, dashed border

Figure 3-15   A solid border that complements the colors in the picture

Creating Powerful Pictures

Now that you're familiar with the power of the Picture Tools Format tab in PowerPoint 2007, let's walk through a few ways you can use your new knowledge.

PowerPoint 2007 presentations offer you a number of preset options that help you create your presentations faster. Use these options, along with Themes, located on the Design tab, and you'll quickly progress in designing attention-getting presentations.

Here's a quick tutorial to help you practice some of the things you just learned. Figure 3-16 uses preset options to create a vibrant scene.

1. Open a PowerPoint 2007 presentation.

2. On the Home tab, click New Slide in the Slides command group.

3. Select the Blank layout.

4. Go to the Insert tab.

5. In the Illustrations group, select Picture to add your picture.

6. In the Picture Styles group, select a style from the Picture Styles gallery.

Figure 3-16   An example of using a preset color in the background

7. In the same group, click Picture Border and select a color for your border.

8. Select Picture Effects.

9. Select Reflection and then a reflection variation.

10. Go to the Design tab.

11. Select Background Styles.

12. Choose the Format Background command.

13. From the Fill screen, click Gradient Fill.

14. Select a color from Preset Colors.

15. Save the presentation.

While preset options are excellent for designing presentations quickly, sometimes you'll want to express your individuality with specific colors and

43

A first glance,
a moment to remember

Figure 3-17   Soften a slide to reflect a poignant moment.

44

designs. Let's look at how you can customize your picture for your needs with another simple tutorial. The results are shown in Figure 3-17.

1. Open a PowerPoint 2007 presentation.

2. On the Home tab, select New Slide and then select Title And Content layout.

3. Go to the Insert tab. Select Picture and add your picture.

4. In the Picture Styles command group, select Picture Shape. Select Oval from the Basic Shapes section.

5. Select Picture Effects and then select Accent Color 4, 18 pt Glow from the Glow Variations section.

6. Select Picture Border. Click Weight and select 4 ½ pt line.

7. Go to the Design tab.

8. Select Background Styles.

9. Choose the Format Background command.

10. From the Fill screen, select Gradient Fill.

11. In the Fill section, select Gradient Fill and then select a color from the options.

12. Click Close.

13. In the Title box, type your message.

14. Save your presentation.

Here's another example of a quick, easy way to customize a slide. The slide layouts are an excellent starting point, but your ingenuity can make slides jump off the page to delight, inspire, and humor. Figure 3-18 uses PowerPoint 2007 textures to bring a little fun to this beach scene.

1. Open a PowerPoint 2007 presentation.

2. Select Add Slide and then select the Picture With Caption layout.

3. From the Insert tab, select Picture and add your picture.

4. Go to Picture Styles and select the style you like.

Figure 3-18 A texture background can add to the picture's story.

5. Select Picture Border and change the color of the border.

6. Go to the Design tab.

7. Select Background Styles.

8. Choose the Format Background command.

9. From the Fill screen, select Picture Or Texture Fill.

10. Choose the texture you like.

11. Click Close.

12. Type your message in the Title box and Text box.

In this chapter, you learned how to adjust the brightness, contrast, and color of any picture to create a specific mood, and how to add a style or shape to tell your story more effectively. You also learned the importance of cropping, sizing, and framing pictures to make them pop off the page. Combining all these elements means you'll be able to create strong presentations.

In the next chapter, you'll learn how photo albums help tell your story in the best way possible.

Creating a
Photo Album

Now that you know how to use pictures to their full potential in PowerPoint 2007, you need a way to capture the spirit of your photos in an organized way. The *Photo Album* lets you have a little fun with presenting photos to family and friends. In this chapter, you'll learn about photo albums and album layouts and discover how to create, edit, and add captions to your photos. You can use PowerPoint 2007's themes for consistency throughout your album, and you'll also learn how simple it is to create a black and white photo album for dramatic effect. You'll even learn how to customize your layout by resizing photos and adding text boxes manually.

Creating and editing a photo album in PowerPoint 2007 is easy. You have a number of options and layouts to choose from. You may want to say it with a caption or a title, or perhaps your photograph will tell a story without any words at all. The wonderful thing about the Photo Album feature is that you get to display your photos the way you want to.

Understanding Album Layouts

The Photo Album in PowerPoint 2007 has ready-made layouts to display your photos one at a time, two at a time, or four at a time. You can include a page title or a caption for each photo. From your computer, you can choose how to display pictures in the way that highlights each photo the best.

Determining which layout to use for your photo album depends on what you're communicating. Are you showing pictures from your beach vacation that have a funny story to tell? Insert a text box so you can tell your story quickly and easily. Have a magnificent photo of a beautiful sunrise that tells the story on its own? Then show off the details with no caption at all. You can frame your photo or let it take up the entire slide. It's your choice.

Layouts are essential in displaying your photos with flair. Let's create and lay out your photo album now.

Creating a New Photo Album

PowerPoint 2007 lets you create a new photo album with just a couple of mouse clicks. Follow these steps to create your album:

1. Select the Insert tab.

2. From the Illustrations group, select Photo Album.

3. Click New Photo Album.

Now you'll see a dialog box displaying your Photo Album options. Since you'll be using the Photo Album dialog box (shown next) to design your album, keep the dialog box open until you've made all your selections. Simply follow along as you read through this chapter, selecting the options you like. After inserting captions in "Adding Captions and Text," later in this chapter, you'll create and edit your album, and then you'll create a few albums to see how the options can work together.

The Album Content Section

The Album Content section in the Photo Album dialog box offers you a number of commands. You'll use this section of the dialog box to determine how your photos will appear. Let's look at the different ways you can insert and adjust photographs:

1. Go to the Album Content section.

2. Under Insert Picture From, click File/Disk, as shown on the next page.

THE EASY WAY

Want to add more than one picture at a time? When selecting photos from your folder, press CTRL while you click the photos you want to include. This way you can insert a number of photos at one time.

3. When the Insert New Pictures dialog box appears, select the picture you want to include.

Once you have your pictures in your album, they'll appear in the Pictures In Album field in the Photo Album dialog box. When you highlight one of the photos, it will appear in the Preview field.

You can reorder pictures by clicking the up or down arrow. You can also delete a photo by highlighting the photo and clicking Remove.

Beneath the Preview field, you'll see three sets of commands. These commands let you

- Rotate the picture.

- Adjust the contrast of the photo.

- Adjust the brightness of the photo.

For dramatic effect or simply to display your photos with a new perspective, check the All Pictures Black And White checkbox under Picture Options in the Album Content section and voila! Now your photo album has a striking new look. To change it back, simply uncheck the box.

Using Album Layouts

The Album Layout section in the Photo Album dialog box (shown on the next page) gives you different page layouts, frame shapes, and themes to choose from. Go to the Album Layout section to select the way you want to display your pictures. Here are your options in the Picture Layout field:

- **Fit To Slide**   Your photo will cover the entire slide.

- **1 picture**   Your photo will be centered on the slide.

- **2 pictures**   Your photos will appear side-by-side on the slide.

- **4 pictures**   Your photos will appear four to a page.

- **1, 2, or 4 Pictures With Title**   This layout adds a title to your photos, which are displayed one, two, or four pictures to a page.

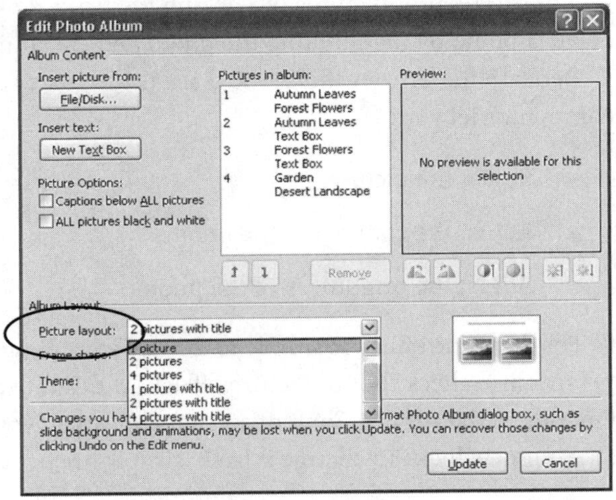

When you choose a Picture Layout other than Fit To Slide, you'll notice the Frame Shape field becomes available. From here, you can select the frame you like. You can choose from among seven frame options:

- Rectangle
- Rounded Rectangle
- Simple Frame, White
- Simple Frame, Black
- Compound Frame, Black
- Center Shadow Rectangle
- Soft Edge Rectangle

When you select either a picture layout or a frame, you'll see a preview to the right. Figure 4-1 shows an example of a Rounded Rectangle frame, whereas Figure 4-2 shows a Compound Frame, Black, and Figure 4-3 displays a Soft Edge Rectangle.

Figure 4-1   A Rounded Rectangle frame

Figure 4-2   A Compound Frame, Black

Figure 4-3   A Soft Edge Rectangle

Using Themes in a Photo Album

Now that you've inserted your photographs, ordered them correctly, and selected a layout, you'll want to present your pictures consistently. The Themes gallery in PowerPoint 2007 is the perfect tool to create the background to tell your story. The gallery offers vibrant colors for a lighthearted feel or more subdued colors to give your slides a more professional air. Either way, the design of each theme will enhance your photos and display them in the best way possible.

Remember, since you are setting a mood and telling a story with photographs, you can use the layout, frame shape, and theme that express your thoughts most effectively.

1.   In the Album Layout section of the Photo Album dialog box, click Browse.

THE EASY WAY

Want to add captions to all the photos in your album? Once you've selected your layout, you can add captions to all your slides. In the Photo Album dialog box, under Picture Options, select Captions Below All Pictures.

2. Review the Themes and select the one you like.

3. Click Select.

Adding Captions and Text

Adding text to your photo album is simple. Just highlight the photo you want to add text to in the Album Content section and then under Insert Text, click New Text Box and then Update. You should now have a new slide with your photo and an empty text box where you can type your caption. To create your own text box on the slide, select the Insert tab and from the Text group, choose Text Box. Then draw your text box on the slide.

Now that you've set up your photo album, let's see what you've created. In the Photo Album dialog box, click Create.

Editing a Photo Album

You can make changes to your photo album using the Edit Photo Album command.

1. Open your PowerPoint 2007 presentation.

2. Go to the Insert tab.

3. Select Photo Album from the Illustrations group.

4. Click Edit Photo Album.

You'll see that the Edit Photo Album dialog box has the same options as the Photo Album dialog box. The only difference is that, instead of the Create command, you'll see the Update command. From here, you can make any adjustments to your photo album.

If you want to make changes to a picture, select your picture, and then go to the Picture Tools Format tab to see the groups and commands you learned about in the previous chapter. You can now edit the photograph as needed.

Displaying Photos in Photo Albums

Now that you've created your photo album, let's look at a few ways to use these options.

1. Go to the Insert tab.

2. From the Illustrations group, select Photo Album.

THE EASY WAY

Need to change a picture quickly? To change a photo in your album, right-click on the photo and select Format Picture. You'll see the Format Picture dialog box that you learned about in Chapter 3. From here, you can adjust the fill, line color, line style, and shadow, along with other options.

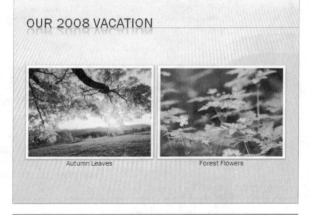

3. Click New Photo Album.

4. In the Album Content section, under Insert Picture From, click File/Disk.

5. From the Insert New Pictures dialog box, select two pictures you want to include in your album.

6. Check the Captions Below All Pictures checkbox.

7. In the Album Layout section, select 2 Pictures With Title.

8. In the Frame Shape field, select Simple Frame, White.

9. Click Browse in the Theme field to select a theme.

10. Click Create.

In Figure 4-4, we selected the Trek theme because of its colors and lines. Now, type in your own title and, if you like, select the captions below the photos and change them as needed. But these are simply captions. If you want to add more text, you'll need to add a text box. Let's change this layout to include text boxes.

Figure 4-4   A 2 Picture With Title layout, captions, and Simple Frame, White

1. Go back to your Photo Album.

2. From the Insert tab in the Illustrations group, click the Photo Album command.

56

3. Select Edit Photo Album.

4. In the Album Content section of the dialog box, highlight the first photo listed in the Pictures In Album field.

5. Click New Text Box under the Insert Text option.

6. Highlight your second photo in the Pictures In Album field.

7. Click New Text Box under the Insert Text option a second time.

8. Uncheck the Captions Below All Pictures checkbox.

9. Click Update.

LEAVES FROM OUR 2008 VACATION

I took this photo as the sun was coming up. The leaves were glistening with dew, and I was surrounded by silence. I wanted to capture a quiet moment in the midst of our busy days.

Figure 4-5   Using the Text Box command for photo albums

In Figure 4-5, you'll see that we now have one picture per slide. Click in the text box to the right of the photo and type your message in the box. The point size of the text will adjust to fit the text box as you type.

The sizes of the photos forced them each onto its own slide. Perhaps you want two photos stacked on top of each other with text boxes to the right. You can manually move your photos and text boxes on the slide. Let's add two new photos, and then move the photos and text where we need them.

From the Insert tab, select the Illustrations group, click Photo Album and then Edit Photo Album. In the Edit Photo Album dialog box, click File/Disk under Insert Picture From. Add two photos to your album and then click Create.

HIGHLIGHT PHOTOS WITH TEXT, TWO AT A TIME

While a four-picture layout option is also available, we wouldn't recommend trying to add text boxes to more than two photos per page. One of the main goals of a photo album is to show off your pictures. Having too many photos on one slide reduces their size and, therefore, their impact. If you need more space, simply add a new slide to your album or let Photo Album move the photos for you.

Figure 4-6   A 2 Picture With Title layout without captions

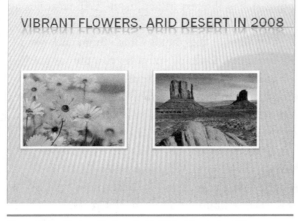

Figure 4-7   Photos displayed at 34% height and width

You should now have two photos side by side on the slide, just as Figure 4-6 does.

Let's resize these pictures so we can add captions.

1. Right-click on the first picture.

2. Select Size And Position.

3. In the Size And Position dialog box, make sure the Lock Aspect Ratio and the Relative To The Original Picture Size checkboxes are selected.

4. On the Size tab in the Scale section, change the Height field to 34%.

5. On the Size tab in the Scale section, change the Width field to 34%.

6. Click Close.

Now, you'll change the second picture the same way by following these steps a second time.

Your slide should look like the one shown in Figure 4-7.

Click on one of the pictures and you'll see the Picture Tools Format tab appear. Select this tab to see your picture options. In the top-right corner of the Arrange group (shown next), you'll see the Align command. Select Align | View Gridlines.

You'll now see some dotted lines on your slide. These are gridlines to help you align objects on your slide. You'll learn more about gridlines in Chapter 10, but for now, you'll simply use them for alignment and remove them when you're done.

1.   Drag your first picture to the left, and align it with the vertical gridlines under your title.

2.   Drag your second picture to the left, place it under your first picture, and align it with the gridlines under your first picture.

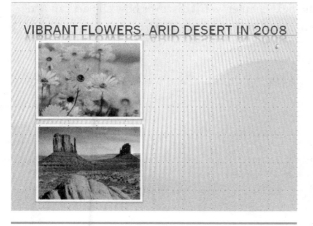

Figure 4-8   Stacking photos using the gridlines for alignment

Your slide will look like the one in Figure 4-8. Now you'll insert the text boxes:

1.   Go to the Insert tab.

2.   In the Text group, click the Text Box command.

3.   Place your cursor in the space to the right of the first photo and drag the width to one of the vertical gridlines.

4.   Type in your message.

5.   In the Text group, click the Text Box command a second time.

6.   Place your cursor in the space to the right of the second photo, and drag the width to one of the vertical gridlines.

7.   Type in your message.

59

VIBRANT FLOWERS, ARID DESERT IN 2008

Line up your text box with one of the horizontal gridlines, and widen it to meet one of the vertical gridlines. Then start typing your message.

Once you have your text typed, you can align the text box with the gridlines and the photos to create a more aesthetic look.

Figure 4-9 Photos and text boxes moved manually and aligned with gridlines using the Align command

Now, align your text boxes using the photos and the gridlines as your guides. Generally, you should center the text box vertically with the photo. When you have the text box where you want it, click one of your photos, select the Picture Tools Format tab; in the Arrange group, select Align and then click View Gridlines. This will remove the gridlines from your presentation. Your slide should look like the one in Figure 4-9.

In this chapter, you learned about what you can do with photo albums. You discovered various album layouts and how to insert photos and captions. You also learned how themes can add some pizzazz to your background and how customizing a layout may be just the right way to display your photos. In the next chapter, you'll discover how clip art can add some spark to your presentations in PowerPoint 2007.

MEMO

Be sure to drag the right side of your text box to a vertical gridline. If you don't do this, your text box will continue resizing to the right as you type, and your text will fall off the slide. You can adjust the size of the text box when you're finished typing.

Working with Clip Art

When you think of adding graphics to a presentation, do you automatically think of using the clip art provided in PowerPoint? That's not unusual. In fact, many people rely solely on clip art for presentations. It's easy to find clip art to suit your needs, and it can illustrate a point in a fun way. That's why people use clip art in a presentation, by the way, to liven up a slide in some way and complement text.

Most clip art comes in the form of illustrations, line drawings, or cartoons, but the term also includes photos, movies, sounds, or website icons. Before clip art became available through the Internet, artwork was actually cut out or "clipped" from books—hence the term *clip art*. The graphic would then be used to accompany the text in magazines, books, or other printed media. Today, of course, clip art can be used digitally on websites, in online newsletters or magazines, and in PowerPoint presentations.

There's more to clip art, however, than just dropping in a cute cartoon from the PowerPoint Clip Art Collection. You can manipulate the colors in the art, twist the art around, find art from Office Online or on the Internet, and use shared collections of clip art from corporate networks. In this chapter, we'll explore all those options and give you a few more tips, too.

Where to Find Clip Art

You can find clip art in several different places. Most people go immediately to the Clip Art Collection, but if you stop there, you just might be missing out on some truly terrific art that can make the difference between a cheesy presentation and an imaginative one. Here are the places to go when you want to find just the right graphic for your presentation.

Clip Art Collections

When you want to add clip art to a slide, the steps are very simple. Go to Insert | Illustrations | Clip Art and simply select the art you want from the pane that opens on the right side of your screen, as shown in Figure 5-1.

This pane is called the *Clip Art pane*. From it, you can access four different types of clip art collections:

- **My Collections**, which holds clips that you create or find and add to your own collection.

- **Office Collections**, which holds clips offered with Microsoft Office 2007.

- **Shared Collections**, which includes clips typically available on shared file servers or common workstations. A network administrator must create and export the collection for use.

- **Web Collections**, which are clips available through the Microsoft Office Online collection.

When you use the Clip Art pane, you can enter search terms, tell PowerPoint where to search, and specify the file types you want to look for.

Figure 5-1   The Clip Art pane

Clip Art on Office Online

To access clip art from Office Online, you need to be connected to the Internet. If a search in the Clip Art pane doesn't yield what you're looking for,

THE EASY WAY

Under Search In, most people leave Everywhere selected as the default. To speed up the search process, you can remove the checkmark from that box and choose a specific collection instead. Choosing a specific media file type is also a good idea so you don't wind up with a movie, for example, when you just want a simple piece of clip art.

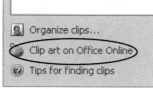

click Clip Art On Office Online at the bottom of the Clip Art pane.

This takes you directly to the Clip Art section of Microsoft Office Online, as shown in Figure 5-2. Here, you can download free clip art, photos, animations, and sounds.

Notice in the left pane the section called *Clip Art Resources.* This is a terrific resource, especially the Clip Art Tips & Help section. It's worth checking out when you have a little time to play around. At the top of the web page is a search function that lets you search all of Office Online for clip art. This search option is far more expansive than the one provided within PowerPoint, so this is a great place to look for additional clip art if you don't find what you need during your initial search. You can also use the Browse Clip Art And Media Categories section of the page to narrow your search into preselected categories, such as Animals, Maps, Travel, and so on.

63

Figure 5-2   Microsoft Office Online devotes an entire section to clip art.

MEMO

PowerPoint will file downloaded clip art into one or more folders based upon the tags provided by Microsoft Office Online. The next time you perform a Clip Art pane search using one of these tags, the clip art will appear.

Selection Basket

Selected items: **1**

Download size: **533 KB**
(1 min @ 56 Kbps)

» Review basket
» Download 1 item

To download items from this site, you'll need to install ActiveX Control for Office Online. It's very fast, and instructions are provided on the site. Once that's done, and you've selected one or more pieces of clip art, a Selection Basket will appear in the left pane as shown here.

THE EASY WAY

If you're searching for clip art and decide that you want to download all the clip art from a single Office Online page, don't bother selecting photos one by one. Instead, click Select Page in the bottom-left corner of the search results. All items on the page will be selected and placed in your Selection Basket for download. The Select Page option will change to Deselect Page; click it to deselect those items so you can move on in your search.

Follow these steps to download the clip art:

1. Click Download (1) Item(s). (The actual text will vary depending on how many items you've chosen.)

2. From the Download screen, click Download Now.

3. Click Open.

Be patient—the download might take a while. When complete, the downloaded item(s) will appear on your hard drive under My Collections in the Downloaded Clips folder of the Clip Organizer, as shown in Figure 5-3. Read "How PowerPoint Organizes Your Clips" to learn more about the Clip Organizer.

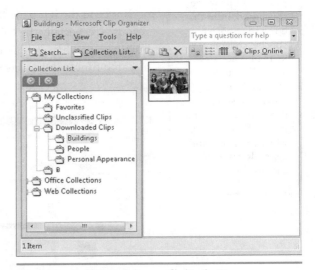

Figure 5-3   Downloaded clips are filed in the My Collections folder.

Online Searches

While Microsoft Office Online might well provide you with the clip art you're seeking, the site doesn't always have what you need. In those situations, perform an online search to try and find what you need. Just use your browser and search engine (such as Google or Yahoo!) and enter the search terms for the type of item you're seeking. One word of caution: Be sure that anything you download from a site other than Microsoft Office Online doesn't have any copyright restrictions. Many sites offer free clip art, but some have specific rules for how you use that clip art. For example, some sites might allow you to download clip art for personal use but not for corporate use. Don't ever assume that you won't get caught using unauthorized clip art! You never know when the creator of that clip art might be sitting in an audience watching your presentation.

Creating Your Own Clip Art

You can create your own clip art, so if you're not finding what you want in any of your searches, then maybe it's time to put on the creativity hat and just make what you want. You can create clip art in two primary ways: You can draw what you want and scan it into your computer, or you can create

HOW POWERPOINT ORGANIZES YOUR CLIPS

PowerPoint has another item that sounds similar to the Clip Art pane: The Clip Organizer. Although the Clip Organizer houses many of the same clips you can find using the Clip Art pane, it's actually the location on your hard drive where PowerPoint *stores* clips for you. It's also a great place to gather and store your own photos, animations, videos, and other media files along with the automatically stored clips from Office Online or elsewhere.

As you add new items to your collections, the Clip Organizer stores them for you and even lets you apply keywords to the clips for easy searching. It sorts items into the categories you find in the Clip Art pane. Because the Clip Organizer is located on your hard drive, you can open and use the clips independent of any Microsoft Office program. Just type **Clip Organizer** into the Start Search box in Vista and click Microsoft Clip Organizer in the results to open it.

The first time you open the Clip Organizer, let it scan your computer for photos and other media files so it can organize files from your hard drive into separate collections. Files will remain in their original locations; PowerPoint just creates shortcuts to them

so you can quickly preview, open, or insert a file. You can also do this at any time if you have been using PowerPoint for a while. Just follow these steps:

1. Click the Organize Clips link at the bottom of the Clip Art pane.

2. Click File In The Favorites – Microsoft Clip Organizer dialog box.

3. Click Add Clips To Organizer, and then click Automatically.

4. In the Add Clips To Organizer dialog box, click Options. The process will take a few minutes.

5. In the Auto Import Settings dialog box, select or clear the checkboxes for the folders you want the clips to be organized into.

6. Click Catalog.

7. Click OK.

The entire process might take several minutes, but you can still work on your presentation as the Organizer toils in the background.

art using a graphics program such as Microsoft Paint, which is included with Windows Vista, or Adobe Photoshop, which is an example of a separate program you can purchase.

Before you begin, be sure you know how to perform basic tasks in your graphics program such as choosing colors, filling shapes, and selecting tools to draw with. Using a graphics program isn't the easiest thing in the world if you don't practice, so give yourself a break if things aren't turning out exactly the way you want them the first time around. The more you play and create, the easier it will become to create exactly the clip art you want.

The tools you will typically use when creating clip art are

- The paint bucket
- Line drawing tool
- Pencil or freehand drawing tool
- Airbrush
- Shapes, such as oval, circle, square
- Color chart

Once you're ready, the sky is the limit. Create a simple housing scene, for instance, by using the rectangle shape for house frames, the line drawing tool for roofs, oval and circle shapes for trees or flowers, and coloring tools as desired. Once your drawing is complete, save it to your hard drive as a graphic file (GIF, TIF, JPG, for example).

Then, to add the new clip art to your Clip Organizer, Windows Vista users can follow these steps:

1. Open the Clip Organizer. (To open the Clip Organizer, type **Clip** in the Windows Vista Start Search box, and then click Microsoft Clip Organizer to open it.)

2. Select File | Add Clips To Organizer.

MEMO

Want a transparent background in your clip art? Save the graphic as a new image, and then use the transparent feature in your graphics program to turn the background transparent. Resave the new graphic to your hard drive. You can add drop shadows the same way; simply resave your graphic with different names and apply the various features you want.

MEMO

Only vector art can be easily manipulated. Most clip art graphics are *vector art*, which is built in layers using lines, curves, and shapes, but photographs and clip art that have been scanned into a computer typically are not. If you're having trouble manipulating a graphic, it's probably because it is not vector art and cannot be manipulated. Most downloaded clip art has not been saved in a vector format, however. Some Microsoft clip art can be manipulated, but generally you can't tweak much clip art from other sites unless the site specifies that you can.

3. Select On My Own.

4. Locate the clip art and then click Add.

Manipulating Clip Art

Once you have the type of clip art you need, you might still find it requires some tweaking. For example, maybe you found the perfect illustration of a cat but the cat is a weird green color and you would prefer a black cat. In this section, we'll show you how to manipulate clip art in different ways to help you get the exact graphic you want.

Most of the time before you can manipulate a piece of clip art, you will need to separate it into layers. That's because most clip art contains multiple colors and images that are grouped into a single scene to create the final piece of clip art. For example, in Figure 5-4, the sky behind the volleyball players is a light blue. If you wanted to change the sky color to dark blue, you must ungroup the entire graphic in order to select only the piece of the graphic containing the sky color.

Figure 5-4   Volleyball scene with a light blue sky in background

Note that if you do not see Edit Picture in the shortcut menu, your object can't be converted to a Microsoft Office drawing object.

To ungroup a graphic, follow these steps:

1. Right-click the graphic.

2. Click Edit Picture from the shortcut menu. If you see a warning that the graphic is an imported picture instead of a group, click Yes to convert it to a Microsoft Office drawing object.

3. Right-click the graphic again.

Link

The Clip Art Book: A Compilation of More Than 5,000 Illustrations and Designs, by Gerard Quinn, Gramercy, 1992.

67

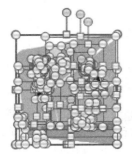

4. Select Group | Ungroup. The graphic should display similarly to the one shown here.

5. Click outside the graphic to reduce all the grouping clutter in your graphic.

6. Now, select the piece of the graphic that you want to alter and make changes as desired.

In our example, we will be changing the sky color so we've selected the sky portion of the graphic. Steps for changing clip art colors are in the next section.

Change Color in Portions of a Graphic

To change colors in certain portions of a graphic, follow these steps:

1. Select the portion of the graphic where the color should be changed.

2. Go to the Drawing Tools Format tab. Click Shape Fill.

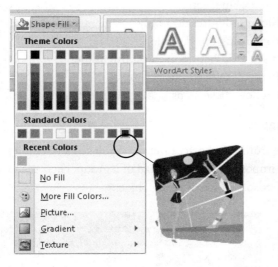

3. Select a new color from the color palette provided (Theme, Standard, or Recent Colors).

The graphic will now reflect the new color you've chosen. Figure 5-5 shows a much darker sky now than the sky shown in Figure 5-4; that's because we applied a new dark blue color to the sky.

Change the Look and Feel of the Entire Graphic

If you prefer to change the entire look of the graphic, and don't want or need to manipulate pieces of it, it's very simple to do. You can change

Figure 5-5   Volleyball scene with dark blue sky in background

the overall color, add 3D rotation, background fill, and more to your graphics before you ungroup them. While this method doesn't allow you to apply changes to portions of the graphic, it does give you an option for making a unique graphic for your presentation.

To change the overall look of a graphic, follow these steps:

1. Right-click the graphic.

2. From the shortcut menu, select Format Picture.

The Format Picture dialog box will appear with Picture already selected in the left pane, as shown in Figure 5-6.

In the left pane, you'll find many other options, however. As you select different options, the right pane will change in relation to the chosen item. We'll briefly review each option so you understand what can be accomplished; we recommend playing with each option so you can see how even minor adjustments to a graphic can make a big difference.

Picture

With the Picture option selected, you can recolor the graphic, change its brightness or contrast, or reset the graphic to its original look.

- Click the Recolor button to select from preset color variations.

- Slide the handle or use the up and down arrows to change brightness and contrast.

69

Format Picture

Fill
Line Color
Line Style
Shadow
3-D Format
3-D Rotation
Picture
Text Box

Picture

Recolor:
Brightness: 0%
Contrast: 0%
Reset picture

Close

Figure 5-6   The Format Picture dialog box allows you to make multiple changes to your graphic.

MEMO

When you're finished making changes, click Close in the Format Picture dialog box for the changes to be applied to your graphic.

MEMO

When using Picture Or Texture Fill, try playing with the Stretch Options. This allows you to move the background to the right or left, or up and down. A 30 percent stretch to the left, for example, gives you a background and graphic similar to the one shown above. Stretch will work on some things and not others, so if it doesn't work on one item, try it on another.

Fill

This option allows you to add or change background colors in your graphic.

- Select No Fill to remove backgrounds.

- Select Solid Fill | Color to see a list of color options. You can also change the background transparency by sliding the handle or using the up and down arrows next to Transparency.

- Select Gradient Fill to select from a variety of gradient color options, types, and directions.

- Select Picture Or Texture Fill to add a picture or preset texture to your graphic. You can use pictures from your own collection or the PowerPoint Clip Art Collection. Select Include Content From Office Online to broaden your options. To make texture options appear larger in the graphic, deselect Tile Picture As Texture.

- Select Slide Background Fill to make your graphic blend seamlessly with your slide.

Line Color

You can line your graphics with a solid or gradient line using this option, as well as change line colors and transparency.

Line Style

When you add lines to a graphic, you can manage the width, type, and style of the line using this option. Play with the Cap and Join types to modify the look of the edge or corners of the line. You won't be able to add arrows to a graphic that you've outlined using this option, but if you're just working with a single line shape, this is where you would go to add arrows to a straight line.

Shadow

Want your graphic to cast a shadow? Select this option, and choose from either Preset options or set the shadow yourself using the Transparency, Size, Blur, Angle, and Distance features. One way to make a shadow stand out: Change its color using the Color button.

3-D Format

When you apply a 3D format to a graphic, it can make your graphic pop off the page. This option is really that terrific when working with cartoons, but try it anyway if you're looking for a way to make a graphic stand out. Sometimes this option can make a simple graphic look like a very cool button. With 3-D Format selected, you can choose from Bevel, Depth, Contour, and Surface options.

HOW GRADIENT STOPS WORK

Gradient stops sound like something fancy but are really just what the name says: They tell PowerPoint where to stop various gradient colors so the next color can begin. Although most people assume that gradients only come in two colors, you can actually have up to ten gradient colors within a graphic.

Each gradient stop has a color associated with it, as well as a stop position and transparency option. The stop position is what limits the particular gradient stop to a specific location in the graphic; transparency dictates how bright or muted that portion of the gradient will be. In Figure 5-7, you can see a variety of gradients applied to the background of the volleyball scene. These were applied by adding ten gradient stops and applying a different color, position, and transparency to each.

To add gradient stops to a graphic, right-click the graphic and click Format Picture. In the Format Picture dialog box, click Add. Our recommendation is to add color first using the Color button, and then set the stop position by sliding the Stop Position handle or using the up and down arrows. Set transparency in the same way. Go ahead and play with this—you'll be pleasantly surprised at how easy it is to add multiple colors to your graphics.

Figure 5-7   In this enlargement of the volleyball scene, you can see numerous gradations in the background.

3-D Rotation

This is a fun option and very useful in PowerPoint. Turn a graphic sideways, or make it lie down on the slide; you can choose from 25 different preset options. Plus, you can manually change the rotation using the X, Y, and Z Rotation buttons. If you want text to remain flat, be sure to select Keep Text Flat. To move a graphic up or down minutely, use the up and down arrows in the Object Position, Distance From Ground box.

Text Box

When you use Word Art (or other kinds of text, too) in your presentation, you can select this option to change the text's alignment, direction, auto fit, and margin aspects. The feature you'll probably use the most is Text Direction. You can make your text lie horizontally, stack it, or rotate it 90 or 270 degrees as shown here.

Edit Points in a Graphic

Sometimes, you might want to change the sizing or shapes in part of your graphic. In Figure 5-8, for example, the left graphic shows sky, ocean, and sand in original proportions. The right graphic, however, shows the sand at an angle to the ocean above it. The sand portion was decreased by editing its points within the graphic.

Figure 5-8   Various aspects of a graphic can be resized by editing the points within it.

To edit points within your graphic, first ungroup the graphic as explained earlier in "Manipulating Clip Art." Then follow these steps:

1.   Right-click the section of the graphic that you want to edit.

2.   From the shortcut menu, click Edit Points. The section will now be outlined in red, with black handles of differing sizes.

3.   Using your mouse, grab a black handle and pull it to its new location.

You can repeat the process multiple times until the section is modified to your liking.

"Wash out" a Graphic

When you use graphics in PowerPoint, you don't want them to overwhelm the audience and distract from your message. However, sometimes the perfect graphic is just too bright to be used effectively in a presentation. In cases like this, try "washing out" the graphic. This process makes a bright graphic more

73

subtle, and it might be just what you need. Figure 5-9 shows the difference between an original graphic and a copy of it washed out using the light variation Background Color 2 Light.

Figure 5-9 Graphics can be muted by applying a simple wash to them.

To wash out a graphic, follow these steps:

1. Right-click the graphic.

2. Select Format Picture. Select Picture.

3. Do one of the following:

   ■ Click Recolor and select one of the Color Modes or Variations.

   ■ Change brightness or contrast using the corresponding sliding handles or up and down arrows.

Arranging Clip Art Objects on Your Slide

Once your clip art objects look the way you want them to, you can drop them into your slides. Remember to follow the design principles explored in Chapter 1, and then follow these tips for arranging clip art as needed.

MEMO

When you're working with some pieces of clip art, you might need to save the art as a picture in order to apply wash out techniques. If you can't access the Picture tools in the Format Shape dialog box, this is most likely the problem. Right-click the graphic and click Save As Picture, and then save the graphic in the file format you prefer.

When you paste clip art onto a slide, you might decide to resize it quickly by using the sizing handles on the art. Be careful; this sometimes causes *pixelization*, which is when the curves of lines in your graphic take on a stair-stepped appearance. You can often avoid this problem by saving the art to your hard drive and resizing it using a graphics program. When the resizing is complete, add it to your slide from its location on the hard drive.

Use Alignment Options

There are some quick ways to position clip art and other graphics on your slide. One feature you need to understand is alignment. With a few mouse clicks, you can align graphics up, down, horizontally, and in other ways. To find the alignment options, first select multiple graphics and then go to the Home tab. Select Drawing | Arrange | Align and choose from ten different alignment options.

Use Order Options

When you have graphics placed on top of one another that need to be moved, you have two different methods for rearranging them. The first is through the Selection Pane, as shown in Figure 5-10, which is accessed through the Arrange group on either the Drawing Tools Format tab or the Picture Tools Format tab.

With the selection pane, you can see a list of every single object on your slide, including text. Just click the item in the list that you want to move, and use the up and down arrows at the

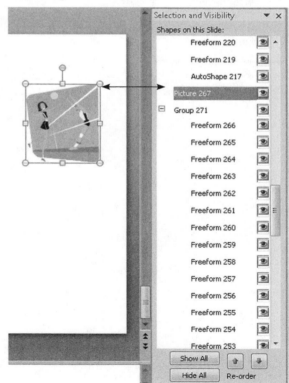

Figure 5-10   The Selection Pane

THE EASY WAY

Go to Home | Drawing | Arrange and select an order option: Bring To Front, Send To Back, Bring Forward, or Send Backward. Bring To Front and Send To Back move items all the way to the front or back, respectively, whereas Bring Forward or Send Backward moves items one step at a time.

bottom of the pane to reorder the object you've selected. However, the second way is our favorite method, so see The Easy Way.

In this chapter, you discovered many different ways to work with clip art. Don't be timid about playing with clip art. You'll find that the more familiar you become with the features covered in this chapter, the easier it will be to create the perfect graphics for your presentations. In the next chapter, we'll explain how to work with tables in PowerPoint 2007.

Working with Tables

Maybe you don't think of a table as a graphic presentation tool, but we sure do. Purists might say tables are simply used to lay out information graphically, but they aren't considering the fact that information within tables can be animated in PowerPoint (more on that in Chapter 12) or can be changed into pictures and, therefore, become graphics in and of themselves.

The bottom line is that tables are a wonderful tool for displaying information; you can compile information from a variety of sources and lump it all together into a single table that clearly outlines every detail. Easy to understand and use, tables can be added to a presentation through either an automatic process or a custom design.

If you've got a presentation that seems heavy on bullets, consider using a table. Tables are a great way to break up the monotony of bulleted page after bulleted page, and the effects and options available in PowerPoint 2007 can make your tables look sharp and professional. Although you might not have considered using tables as a graphic presentation tool, you can design tables in new ways that will have you thinking twice about the entire idea.

In this chapter, we'll explore how tables are created and edited. We'll also show you how to use color effectively, as well as how to use the two different tabs that will appear when you create a table: the Table Tools Design tab and the Table Tools Layout tab.

Creating Tables

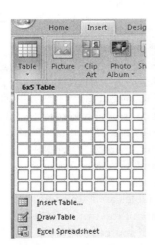

You can add a table to your presentation in one of two ways: by drawing it or by using a simple dialog box to specify the number of rows and columns. Both methods are accessed via the Insert tab in the Tables group. Either method is fine.

To add text to the table, click within a cell and then start typing. To change the font, font color, or font size of the text, highlight the text and use the Font group on the Home tab to make the desired changes. You can also change text from cell to cell by using the Paragraph group tools on the Home tab. In individual cells or throughout the table (highlight specific areas to apply changes universally), you can

- Align text differently.
- Add bullets.
- Add numbers.
- Change list levels.
- Change line spacing.

Add Rows or Columns

After you've created the table on your slide, if you discover that you need an additional row, you can add one by highlighting a row and right-clicking. From the shortcut menu, select Insert | Insert Rows Above or Insert Rows

THE EASY WAY

To add a table to your presentation, click the slide, and then go to Insert | Table and select the number of table rows and columns by dragging the cursor across until you've selected the desired number (as shown above). Click in the final cell and the table will appear on your slide.

THE EASY WAY

To add a single row to the bottom of your table, click the last cell in the last row and press TAB on your keyboard.

	Cut
	Copy
	Paste
A	Font...
	Bullets ▸
	Numbering ▸
	Hyperlink...
	Synonyms ▸
	Insert ▸
	Delete Rows
	Delete Columns
	Merge Cells
	Split Cells...
	Select Table
	Format Shape...

	Insert Columns to the Left
	Insert Columns to the Right
	Insert Rows Above
	Insert Rows Below

MEMO

You can also add or delete more rows or columns using the Rows & Columns group on the Table Tools Layout tab.

Below. You can add more columns in almost the same way. Just highlight a column and then right-click. Select Insert | Insert Columns To The Right or Insert Columns To The Left, as shown above.

Delete Rows or Columns

When you need to delete a column or row within a table, just right-click in a cell in the desired row or column. Then click Delete Rows or Delete Columns from the shortcut menu depending upon your goal.

Merge Cells

Sometimes you might need to combine the cells in parts of a table to present the information more clearly. While you can use the Table Tools Layout tab to merge cells, you can also merge adjoining cells in rows or columns by following these steps:

1. Highlight the cells you want to merge.

2. Right-click the highlighted area.

3. Click Merge Cells.

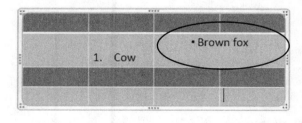

Figure 6-1 shows an example of a merged cell

Figure 6-1 A merged cell can help you present information more effectively.

with unmerged cells above and below it. If you need to split a cell, follow the steps just described but click Split Cells in Step 3 instead. In the Split Cells dialog box, specify the number of rows or columns and then click OK.

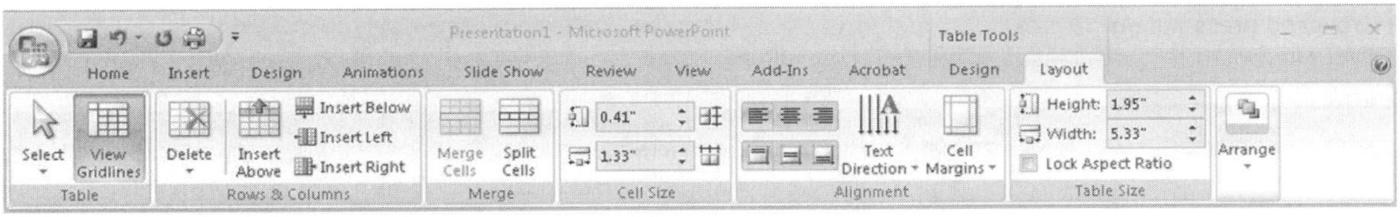

Figure 6-2   The Table Tools Layout tab

The Table Tools Layout Tab

Earlier in this chapter, we mentioned the Table Tools Layout tab as a method for inserting rows and columns or merging cells. You can also do a few more things on this tab that are worth noting from a graphics perspective. Figure 6-2 shows the Table Tools Layout tab.

TABLE DO'S AND DON'TS

Because of updates in PowerPoint 2007, you'll discover some compatibility issues with earlier versions of PowerPoint. If your presentation will be used by people who don't have PowerPoint 2007, you should be aware of problems that can arise concerning tables when people view presentations in earlier versions. As you build your tables, think about the audience and how the presentation will be viewed. Then review these Do's and Don'ts to be certain that your presentation can be viewed easily by your entire audience.

Do...

■ Use No Style, Table Grid, or No Style, No Grid under Best Match For Document.

■ Use No Style, Table Grid, or No Style, No Grid when working with backgrounds.

■ Use a Quick Style under Light, Medium, and Dark when working with backgrounds.

Don't...

■ Use All Quick Styles under Best Match For Document.

■ Use background fills as a shape.

■ Apply a Quick Style with a background shape.

■ Use visual effects (shadows, bevels, and so on) or apply pictures, gradients, and texture fills to cells or text.

■ Use WordArt on text in table cells.

■ Change text orientation.

asdfsdfasdas dfasdfsadfsa dfasdfadsfas	asdf sdfa sdas dfas dfsa dfsa dfas dfad sfas

Figure 6-3   Customizing margins can make your text display more effectively within a table.

Cell Size

While you can certainly grab the edges of cells or the entire table to drag to resize the given item, you can also change the size of these items incrementally by using the Cell Size command group. (You can also use the Table Size group.) These options are particularly helpful when you have a table that needs to fit in a very specific location on your slide. This command group also offers you the options of equally distributing the height and width of rows or columns. Just click Distribute Rows or Distribute Columns and PowerPoint does the rest to be sure your columns and rows are perfectly sized.

Alignment

You can customize the text margins of the cells in your table using the Cell Margins commands in the Alignment group. If the text is bumping against the edges of a cell, for instance, these commands can help you make the text more appealing to readers. You can select from preset options or click Custom Margins to determine your own margins. In the Cell Text Layout dialog box, just specify the internal margins that you want. Figure 6-3 shows the difference between original text (left cell) and text placed within customized margins (right cell).

You can also change the direction of text within the table cells by using the Text Direction commands in the Alignment group. Highlight multiple cells to change text direction in more than one cell.

Table Size

If you need to keep your table at a certain aspect ratio to make it work correctly on your slide, the Table Size command group is the place to get that done. Just place a check mark in the box next to Lock Aspect Ratio.

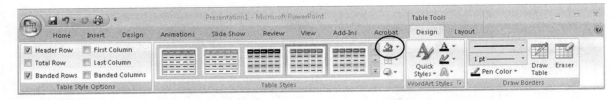

Figure 6-4 The Table Tools Design tab

The Table Tools Design Tab

When you insert a table in PowerPoint 2007, the colors default to a combination of colors based on the theme you have chosen for the presentation. The header row will usually be a darker shade, whereas the rows below will alternate in lighter shades. Columns are typically delineated by simple white lines.

This color scheme and format, however, might not be exactly what you need for your presentation. It might match your theme, but maybe you want to add more punch to your presentation. That's when you'll want to use the Table Tools Design tab, as shown in Figure 6-4. From this tab, you can change a variety of styles and colors associated with your table.

Use Color to Make Your Point

Color is a major factor in giving your table the impact it needs to capture audience attention. You can keep the basic style of your table so it matches your overall presentation theme, yet easily changes the colors within it. As you play with color in a table, consider which pieces of information need to stand out for your audience and which pieces can be used more in the background.

For example, perhaps you want the header row and any subsection rows of your table to pop out in bright yellow so the audience can easily see where new information rests within a table. Or maybe you want alternate color in columns or rows so the audience can identify different pieces of information in the table simply. Some presentations, on the other hand, might work better with a table that is completely uniform in color.

MEMO

Don't confuse the Table Tools Design tab with the standard Design tab on the Ribbon. The Table Tools Design tab commands allow you to change table formatting; the standard Design tab lets you make design changes to all other aspects of your presentation.

MEMO

The Table Styles Gallery works in conjunction with the Table Style Options group, which is explained later in this chapter.

To change the entire look of a table into one that uses uniform color, follow these steps:

1. Click the edge of the table.

2. In the Table Styles group, click Shading.

3. Click a color from the Theme, Standard, or More Fill Colors groups.

The entire table will change to the color you've selected. To change a color in a single row or column, simply highlight the row or column and then follow Steps 2 and 3.

Working with Table Styles

The Table Styles group offers you other options beyond merely coloring your table. For example, you can add or remove borders for cells or your entire table by using Border commands. You can also apply effects to your table from this group and instantly change the table style by using the Table Styles Gallery.

The Table Styles Gallery

Within the Table Styles group is the Table Styles Gallery. This is a group of preset tables that you can choose from to apply an overall look and feel instantly to your table. Click the More button (it looks like a down arrow with a line above it) to see the entire selection of styles available for your table.

When the Gallery opens, you'll see several different style categories. The first, Best Match For Document, is PowerPoint's recommendation for table styles that will work well within the theme that you've chosen. The remaining categories,

83

The primary Borders command within the Table Styles group changes its title depending upon the current option chosen for the table.

Light, Medium, and Dark, are all variations of the Best Match category. At any time, you can clear the options to return to a simple table with no color by clicking Clear Table in the Gallery.

All About Borders

To apply borders to your entire table, click the outside edge of the table and choose the Borders command and then choose All Borders. If you need to change the border of a particular cell or group of cells, highlight the cells, and then select or deselect the border command desired (Inside, Outside, Top, Left, and so on). Figure 6-5 shows a table with some borders selected and others deselected.

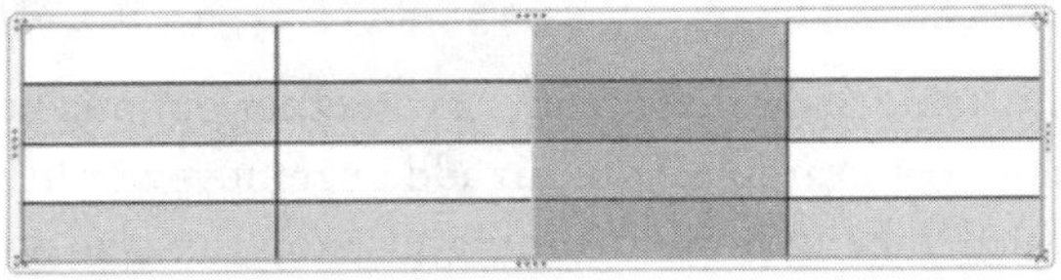

Figure 6-5   A table with All Borders initially selected, and then a center column highlighted, and Left Border deselected

If you want to change the border look from the solid line default, select Draw Borders | Pen Color and click the option you prefer. Then, using the mouse (which now appears as a pen on your screen) draw over the borders you want to change. The borders will instantly appear in the new border style you have selected. You can apply multiple border styles within a table by using this command, as shown in Figure 6-6. If you want to change the width of the border lines, you can do that using the Pen Weight command. Just select a new weight from the options provided.

Need to change the color of the border? Simply choose a different Pen Color in the Draw Borders group, and then draw over the borders that you want to change. By the way, you can erase borders

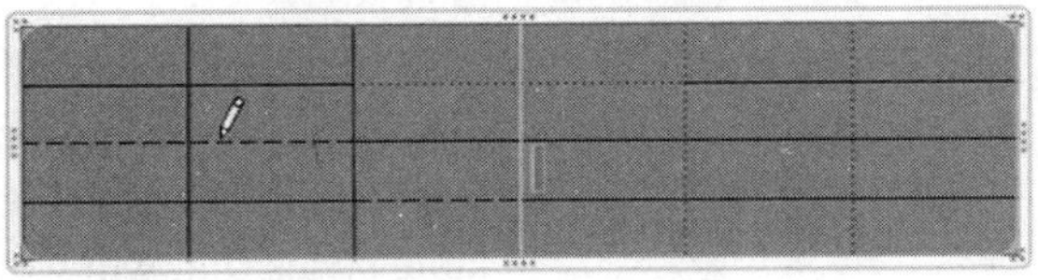

MEMO

Before you change border aspects, be certain that you have selected the final Table Style. If you change the table style, you will almost always lose any border changes that you've applied.

Figure 6-6   A table with multiple border style options

in a table by using the Eraser command in the Draw Borders group. Just click it, and then use your mouse to erase any borders you don't like.

Adding Effects

Some of the real fun with table graphics comes with adding effects to your table. These are all located on the Table Tools Design tab. You can typically apply effects to a single cell to help it pop out for viewers, or you can apply them to the entire table. Although applying effects to an entire table generally isn't recommended because it can make the table more difficult to read, it can sometimes work. Some effects, however, will apply in a particular way to your table regardless of whether you're trying to apply the effect to a single cell or the entire table, so you're going to have to play around a little bit to see how each effect impacts your table.

You can apply three main effects to a table: Cell Bevel, Shadow, and Reflection.

With *Cell Bevel*, you can apply a bevel effect to individual cells in a table. This effect has the most impact when you need to spotlight a particular area of a table.

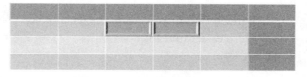

To apply Cell Bevel, select the cells you want to spotlight; then go to the Table Styles command group, select Effects | Cell Bevel, and then choose a bevel option.

Shadow, on the other hand, applies to the entire table. You can choose from inner and outer shadow options.

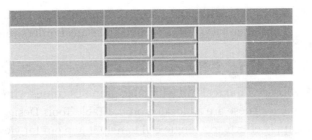

Reflection, too, applies to the entire table.

You can use both Shadow and Reflection effects in conjunction with Cell Bevel effects.

Understanding Table Style Options

The Table Style Options group is used in conjunction with the Table Styles Gallery. Select or deselect a Table Style Option, and the instant styles shown in the Table Styles Gallery will change accordingly. The options are

■ **Header Row**   Specially formats the top row of a table.

■ **Total Row**   Applies to the bottom row of the table. This option tallies the column totals and displays them.

■ **Banded Rows**   Formats even and odd rows differently so they are easy to read.

■ **First Column**   Specifically formats the first column in a table.

■ **Last Column**   Specially formats the last column in a table.

■ **Banded Columns**   Formats even and odd columns differently to make them easier to read.

MEMO

Need to remove the header line below the first row? Go to Table Style Options and deselect Header Row.

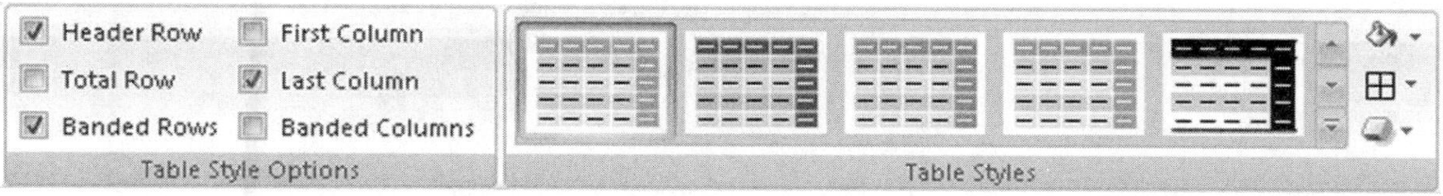

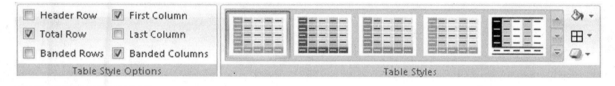

Figure 6-7   Table Style Options chosen: Header Row, Banded Rows, and Last Column

Figures 6-7 and 6-8 show how different Table Style Options impact Gallery choices.

This chapter covered a lot of ground concerning the use of tables in Power-Point. You learned how to add color, use Table Style Options and Effects, work with Table Styles, and use a variety of tools to make your tables stand out and deliver information in a clear, concise manner. In the next chapter, we'll show you how to use WordArt to make your point.

Figure 6-8   Table Style Options chosen: Total Row, First Column, and Banded Columns

Using WordArt to Make Your Point

WordArt in PowerPoint 2007 gets your message to your audience in an exciting way. Sure, they're just words, but when you need to get your point across quickly and effectively in literally seconds, you can depend on WordArt to create a lasting impression.

Remember, your PowerPoint 2007 presentations are telling a story and conveying a message. You want to use every opportunity to make sure those viewing the presentation are captivated enough to remember what you said. If they don't find at least one "memorable moment," you'll feel like you wasted your time. So whether you're presenting to family or friends, a group of coworkers or potential clients, you can use numerous features in PowerPoint 2007 to keep your presentation at the front of your audience's minds.

In this chapter, you'll discover a variety of ways that WordArt can enhance your presentation, including applying fill, outlines, shapes, and effects. You'll also learn how to align, rotate, and flip the art for maximum effect and how to use a dialog box that lets you make changes from one location.

Getting Started with WordArt

To get to WordArt, follow these steps:

1. Click the Insert tab.

2. Go to the Text group and select the WordArt command.

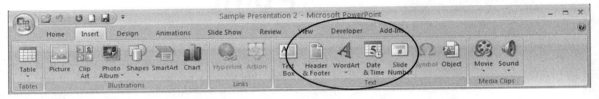

3. Click Fill – Text 2, Outline – Background 2.

Your WordArt will appear like what's shown in Figure 7-1. From here, you can type in your message and customize your text with

- **Text Fill**   Lets you fill the text with a solid color, gradient, texture, or picture.

- **Text Outline**   Lets you define the text with the color, width, and style of line for the outline.

A WORD ON WORDS

WordArt is simply designed to help make your words memorable, but starting with strong, active verbs is the best way to make your presentation pop off the page. Active verbs take charge of the situation—or the slide—by giving the subject of your sentence the action directly. Look at this sentence:

The ball was thrown by the quarterback.

This sentence is passive, showing the ball being thrown. Although this is a perfectly acceptable sentence, it's not the most powerful way to tell your story quickly on a slide. Now look at this sentence:

The quarterback threw the ball.

This sentence shows the subject actively performing the action. The sentence is also shorter and takes less time to read. It helps your storyline along by getting to the point quickly and effectively.

Every time you write a headline on a slide, with or without WordArt, check your verb to make sure you've used the active tense. This evaluation alone can make a significant difference in getting your point across with more pizzazz.

Now, enough of the English lesson.

MEMO

If you want to change the style of your WordArt, select Quick Styles in the WordArt Styles group and apply a style to selected text or to all the text. If you want to remove the WordArt, choose WordArt Styles | Quick Styles | Clear WordArt.

- **Text Effects**   Offers options such as 3D rotation, glow, reflection, or shadow.

WordArt Captivates!

Figure 7-1   Here is one example of a simple WordArt style.

Let's see how applying these options with a few simple clicks can create an eye-catching message.

Adding Fill to WordArt

Once you have added WordArt to a slide, you might decide that the color isn't exactly what you want. It's easy to change it by following these steps:

1. Type your message in the text box, and then highlight the text.

2. Go to the WordArt Styles group.

3. Select the Text Fill command.

4. Hover your cursor over a few colors for a Live Preview of what the text will look like.

5. Choose Red, Accent 2, Lighter 40%.

Figure 7-2 adds some color to the WordArt. Some of your WordArt selections already have some extra effects such as Figure 7-3, which includes a glow effect using Fill – None, Outline – Accent 6, Glow – Accent 6; or Figure 7-4, which applies an inner shadow using Fill – Accent 1, Inner Shadow – Accent 1.

WordArt Captivates!

Figure 7-2   Adding color to a basic WordArt style

WordArt Captivates!

Figure 7-3   A WordArt style with glow effect

WordArt Captivates!

Figure 7-4   A WordArt style with inner shadow

Adding an Outline to WordArt

Outlines can enhance WordArt and make it standout from the background, whether you have a light outline on a dark background or vice versa. Experiment with line weights, colors, and solid or dashed lines, and you'll be able to create powerful presentations. Let's take a look at the difference an outline can make:

1. Select your WordArt.

2. Go to the WordArt Styles group.

3. Select the Text Outline command.

4. Hover your cursor over the colors for a Live Preview.

5. Select Red Accent 2, Darker 50%.

6. Select the Text Outline command.

7. Select Weight. Click the 2¼ point weight to see the effect shown in Figure 7-5.

WordArt Captivates!

Figure 7-5   WordArt with a 2 ¼-point outline

Look at how a few changes in Figure 7-5 can bring new meaning to your slide. You can also add dashes to WordArt to change the meaning even more.

1. Select the WordArt.

2. Click Text Outline.

3. Select Dashes and then select Round Dot.

WordArt Captivates!

Figure 7-6   A dashed line of round dots makes this WordArt airy and light.

Figure 7-6 uses the same 2¼-point line weight, but by adding the dashes, you end up with a much lighter effect and give your message a new meaning.

MEMO

Be careful when applying line weights to WordArt—you don't want the outline to overwhelm the fill. As a general rule, you'll want to contrast or complement the fill color with the outline color to make it pop. Play with the line weights to see what looks best for what you're trying to achieve. You'll also want to check line weights with the size of the WordArt on your slide. Varying sizes may affect legibility.

93

THE EASY WAY

The Quick Styles command gives you a simple way to make changes to WordArt. When you select the WordArt on your slide, you'll see the Quick Styles command in the Drawing group on the Home tab. This gallery is the same one you'll find in the Shape Styles box.

Working with Shape Styles

Although backgrounds are generally considered uneventful in many situations, your background choices can help your WordArt stand out in the midst of a presentation. You'll want to make careful choices in order to use backgrounds effectively. Use the Shape Styles Gallery to quickly insert a background that makes WordArt stand out from the rest of the presentation. We'll briefly explore Shape Styles in this chapter, but you'll learn more about shapes in Chapter 8, "Creating Effective Shapes."

1. Select your WordArt.

2. Select the Drawing Tools Format tab.

3. Go to the Shape Styles group and roll your cursor over the boxed "Abc" letters for a Live Preview of how your WordArt will look.

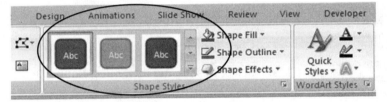

4. Click the down arrow for more options.

5. Select Light 1 – Outline, Colored Fill – Dark 1.

Is Figure 7-7 intense? Yes, it definitely gets attention.

Figure 7-7 Contrasting a dark background with light text

WordArt Captivates!

But you can add one more step to make the WordArt pop even more. Since the original outline was dark, it now blends into the background. Let's change the outline to a lighter color:

1. Highlight the WordArt.

2. Go to Drawing Tools Format tab.

3. From the WordArt Styles group, select the Text Outline command.

4. Select White, Background 1.

5. Select the Text Outline command again.

6. Click Weight.

7. Select 1½ point.

See how the outline in Figure 7-8 draws out the WordArt more? This contrast of dark and light gives the WordArt layers, making it a bit more complex and interesting.

Figure 7-8   A contrasting outline on WordArt

95

THE EASY WAY

To replicate Figure 7-2 easily, go to Text group on the Insert tab and then select WordArt and Fill – Text 2, Outline – Background 2. For the fill, select Red, Accent 2, Lighter 40% using the Text Fill command in the WordArt Styles group.

Applying Text Effects

Text Effects offer several options for making WordArt come alive. Let's look at how the Transform option in WordArt can add movement and excitement. We'll be using Figure 7-2 for these effects.

1. Go to the Drawing Tools Format tab.

2. In the Word Art Styles group, select Text Effects.

3. Select Transform.

4. Under the Wave section, click Double Wave 1.

The wave effect in Figure 7-9 makes the WordArt livelier. Transforming WordArt into something catchy or intense or fun is one of the great things about this command. However, the goal of your presentation is to tell a story, and if the text isn't legible, your message will get lost. So in the midst of your creativity, keep this goal in mind. Here are a few examples for your review.

WordArt Captivates!

Figure 7-9   Double Wave 1 creates movement in WordArt.

Figure 7-10 shows the transform effect called Triangle Up, whereas Figure 7-11 displays the Deflate Inflate effect. Notice how both of these effects can be easily read. The Circle effect and Fade Down effect shown in Figures 7-12 and 7-13, respectively, are more difficult to read. However, when you change the text to a darker color with no outline, as in Figure 7-14, the slide is more legible. This color is Gradient Fill, Accent 6, Inner Shadow Style. Give yourself permission to explore options in WordArt to ensure your message can still be read.

WordArt Captivates!

Figure 7-10   Triangle Up effect

WordArt Captivates!

Figure 7-11   Deflate Inflate effect

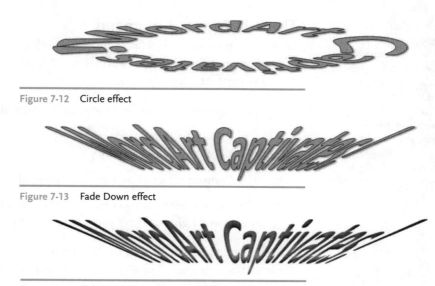

Figure 7-12   Circle effect

Figure 7-13   Fade Down effect

Figure 7-14   Color makes the Fade Down effect more legible.

Working from the Format Text Effects Dialog Box

Want a fast, easy way to refine your
WordArt from one location? No
problem. Click the arrow in the
bottom-right corner of the WordArt
group from the Drawing Tools Format
tab. This will bring up a Format Text
Effects dialog box that lets you make
changes from one handy location.
You can change the text fill, outline,
line style, 3D format and rotation,
along with text box layout, auto fit, and
internal margins.

To make your message jump off the page, consider limiting the number of words you use in WordArt. Brevity, along with the use of active verbs discussed earlier in this chapter, will go a long way toward creating a dynamic presentation.

The 3-D Format Command

Let's take a moment to look at some of the options in the Format Text Effects dialog box, specifically the 3-D Format and 3-D Rotation commands.

3-D Format lets you adjust

- The Bevel effect to make your WordArt look like raised or indented lettering.

- The Depth effect to intensify your WordArt.

- The Contour effect to change the outline of your WordArt.

- The Surface effect so you can select the type of material (i.e., plastic, metal) and lighting effect you want to create.

To see what you can do with the 3-D Format command, let's work with the original slide you created in Figure 7-2. Select Fill – Text 2, Outline – Background 2 from the WordArt group and Red, Accent 2, Lighter 40% from the Text Fill options to re-create Figure 7-2.

1. Click the WordArt to display the Drawing Tools Format tab.

2. Select your WordArt.

3. Click the arrow in the bottom-right corner of the Word Art Styles group.

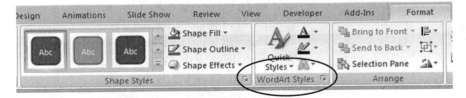

4. In the Format Text Effects dialog box, select 3-D Format.

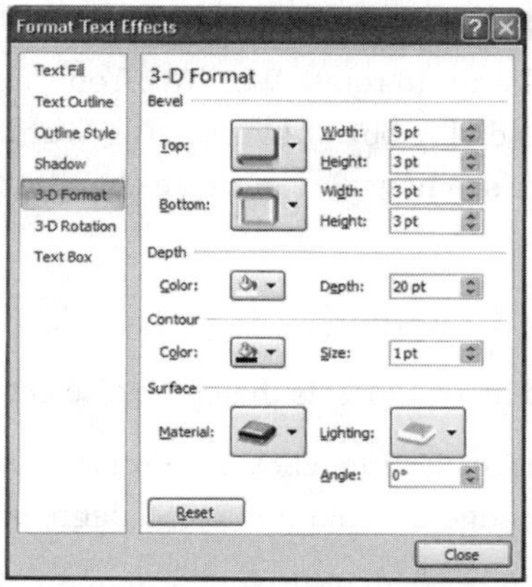

5. In the Bevel section, select the Circle effect.

6. Change Depth to 20 point.

7. Change Contour to 1 point.

8. In the Surface section, select Material.

9. Select Metal in the Standard section.

10. In the Surface section, select Lighting.

11. Select Glow in the Special section.

12. Click Close.

What do you think of Figure 7-15? Can you see how easy it is to create a completely new effect by working with the 3-D Format command options in the Format Text Effects dialog box? There are thousands of ways you can use these options to create the special effect that's exactly right for the message you're communicating.

Figure 7-15 The 3-D Format command can give WordArt a new look and feel.

WordArt Captivates!

The 3-D Rotation Command

Occasionally, you'll want to rotate WordArt. You can do this easily from the Format Text Effects dialog box or by selecting WordArt Styles | Text Effects | 3-D Rotation. Let's see how we can make changes from the Format Text Effects dialog box.

1. Select your WordArt.

2. In the Format Text Effects dialog box, select 3-D Rotation.

3. In the Rotation section, click once on the Left button in the X: option. This will change the rotation to 355 degrees.

4. In the Y: option, click the Down option one time. This will change the rotation to 355 degrees.

5. In the Z: option, click Counter-Clockwise three times for a 15 percent rotation.

6. Click Close.

Figure 7-16 shows an example of rotated WordArt. You can rotate your WordArt in a variety of ways; experiment to see what you can do with 3D rotation.

Figure 7-16   Rotated WordArt

THE EASY WAY

Want an even faster way to rotate WordArt? When the WordArt text box is selected, use the green dot at the top of the text box to rotate the text to the angle you like. As you see in Figure 7-17, simply put your cursor over the dot. Turn to the right or left until you have the desired angle and then release the cursor.

Figure 7-17   WordArt rotation using the text box

The Presets command in the Format Text Effects box also has a variety of rotations to choose from. In the Text section, select Keep Text Flat to flatten out your text, removing the 3D formatting. The Object Position | Distance From Ground command moves rotated WordArt to the left or right.

The Text Box Command

You can make a number of changes to your text box using the Text Box command options in the Format Text Effect dialog box. In the Text Layout section, you can adjust where the WordArt falls inside the text box or rotate the WordArt so it appears sideways or stacked, depending on your needs.

In the Autofit section, you can choose whether you want to resize the shape or the text, or whether you need to apply Autofit to your text at all. The Internal Margin section lets you decide the distance between the WordArt and the edges of the text box. It also lets you decide if you want to wrap text or put it into columns. Let's take a moment to look at this section from within the Format Text Effects dialog box:

1. Select your WordArt.

2. Click the arrow in the bottom-right corner of the WordArt Styles group on the Drawing Tools Format tab.

3. In the Format Text Effects dialog box, select the Text Box option.

4. In the Text Layout section, select Middle for Vertical Alignment.

5. In the Text Direction field, select Rotate All Text 90 Degrees.

101

Now the WordArt in Figure 7-18 is placed on its side and reads like most book titles on a book spine. It may fall off the PowerPoint 2007 slide too, depending on the size of the WordArt. If this is the case, simply drag the overflow portion of the box back onto the slide.

The next section, Autofit, will also help you resize the WordArt to fit the text box. For easier reading, we'll use WordArt that runs horizontally rather than vertically. The Autofit default for WordArt is Resize Shape To Fit Text, which means that the text box adjusts itself to accommodate the WordArt as you type. The text box can be adjusted in two other ways as well. Let's look at both options.

Autofit adjusts either your shape or your text to make it fit for you automatically. Without this, text runs beyond the box. Right-click your WordArt, and then select Format Text Effects. From the Format Text Effects dialog box, select Text Box and then Do Not Autofit and Close. Begin typing within your WordArt text box. Notice how the text falls outside the text box borders and onto the rest of the page, as in Figure 7-19. You may sometimes need to select this option to accomplish a specific task in PowerPoint 2007, but its use is generally rare.

Figure 7-18 WordArt rotated at 90 degrees resembles the spine of a book.

Figure 7-19   WordArt without Autofit falls out of the text box borders.

The other option is to Shrink Text On Overflow. This means that as you type, the text will shrink to fit the box. From the Format Text Effects dialog

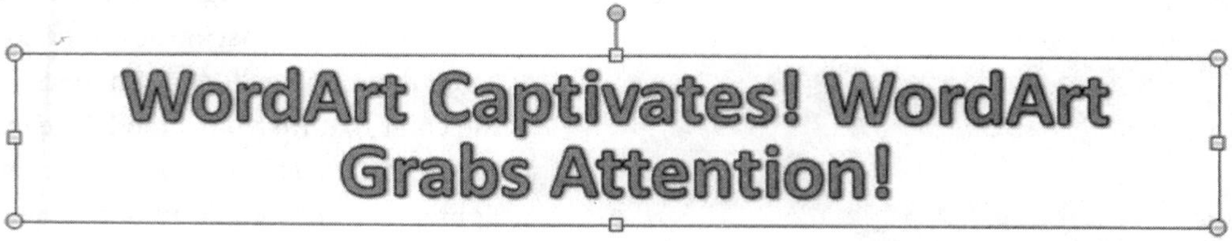

WordArt Captivates! WordArt
Grabs Attention!

Figure 7-20 Using the Shrink Text On Overflow option

box, select Shrink Text On Overflow. Begin typing within your WordArt text box. Figure 7-20 shows the result of the Shrink Text On Overflow option. This WordArt option works well as long as you don't have too many words. Remember earlier we discussed using fewer words in WordArt? The fewer words you use in WordArt, the more powerful your message will be.

The Text Box option in the Format Text Effects dialog box also lets you change the internal margins to give you a bigger background space. Let's say you want to "frame" your WordArt with color. First, let's change WordArt back to its default Autofit option, Resize Shape To Fit Text. Now, let's work with the Internal Margin section of Text Box options.

1. In the Left field, change the margin to 1.5 inches.
2. In the Right field, change the margin to 1.5 inches.
3. In the Top field, change the margin to 1 inch.
4. In the Bottom field, change the margin to 1 inch.
5. Click Close.

Figure 7-21 shows an example of how you can use the text box to create a frame for WordArt.

Did you notice how the text box reshaped itself

WordArt
Captivates!
WordArt
Grabs
Attention!

Figure 7-21 Changing internal margins creates a "frame" for WordArt.

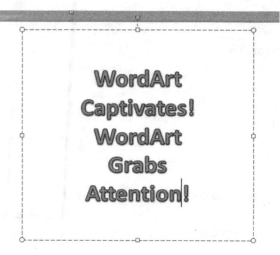

Figure 7-22   Choose a light color for the background to highlight WordArt.

as you were changing the internal margin? Now you have a larger background for color. You can scroll down the gallery of Shape Styles to select the color that fits your mood. The example in Figure 7-22 uses Subtle Effect, Accent 5 for a lighter background. From here, you can adjust the outline to help you frame your WordArt even more.

Using the Arrange Group

Let's look at two Arrange group commands in this chapter: Align and Rotate.

Working with the Align Command

The Align command does a lot of the work for you when it comes to arranging and positioning WordArt on a slide. Use this command fully, and your proficiency will increase as the time you spend moving WordArt decreases.

When you select the Align command, you'll see your command options in the dialog box. The default for this command is Align To Slide, but you can align to the left, right, top, or bottom of the slide as needed. Take a few moments to

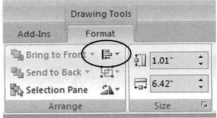

explore these options. You can also move WordArt manually on the slide, but these commands give you plenty of options to choose from.

The View Gridlines and Grid Settings Commands

Two of the most important commands you'll need when positioning WordArt on your slide are View Gridlines and Grid Settings. Both of these help you arrange WordArt manually while ensuring your spacing is consistent. If you've ever worked with PowerPoint in any capacity, you'll know the value of having a grid to place WordArt on in order to achieve an aesthetic, well-arranged slide.

1. On the Drawing Tools Format tab, select the Align command.

2. Select View Gridlines.

Now you'll see dotted vertical and horizontal lines. These lines are for your use only—you'll need to unselect the View Gridlines command before making your presentation.

The second command, Grid Settings, lets you adjust the settings to your preferences. Here's what you'll see when you select this command.

In the Snap To section, you have the option to *snap*, or align, WordArt with the gridlines or to other objects. The default is Snap To Grid, however, you can choose Snap To Other Objects as well or snap to both. In this way, PowerPoint 2007 will do a lot of the work for you.

If you don't like the default grid settings, you can change them by adjusting the Spacing numbers in the Grid Settings section of the Grid And Guides dialog box. This will make the grid squares larger or smaller, depending on your needs.

To show drawing guides on the screen using the Align command, select Grid Settings, and in the Grid And Guides dialog box, go to the Guide

MEMO

Although the Snap To section is designed to help you, you can turn the commands off if you need to align WordArt or other objects manually. Simply uncheck one or both boxes in the Snap To section, and you'll be able to set your items anywhere on the slide.

Settings section and select Display Drawing Guides On Screen. While the vertical and horizontal lines (shown below) are set at zero, you can move them anywhere on the slide to help you align your WordArt with other objects, including drawings, clip art, and so on.

WordArt Captivates!

Rotating and Flipping WordArt

By now, you've learned a lot about rotating WordArt; however, in addition to setting WordArt on its side, the Rotate command lets you flip WordArt upside down. Select Rotate | Flip Vertical. Like the effect? No worries. If you don't like it, simply select Rotate | Flip Horizontal to return your WordArt to your original position.

You can access the Size And Position dialog box you learned about in Chapter 3 by clicking More Rotation Options.

So, what's the most effective way to use WordArt? Sparingly. A little Word-Art goes a long way, so use it only when you need to make a powerful point that you want your audience to remember.

In this chapter, you learned how to add fills, outlines, and effects to Word-Art. You were also introduced to the Format Text Effects dialog box, where you can perform a number of actions to refine and customize your WordArt. And using the Align, Rotate, and Flip commands gives you more control over WordArt. You also were introduced to Shape Styles, which you'll learn more about in Chapter 8.

Creating Effective Shapes

Shapes in PowerPoint 2007 lend themselves to a number of uses for work and play. Whether you need shapes for a flow chart or you simply want to show off the "star" of your family, shapes are a great way to highlight important points, people, and objects in your presentation.

PowerPoint 2007's ready-made shapes are the perfect start for using shapes, but you can also customize a shape to suit your needs. In this chapter, you'll learn when to use shapes, how to add fill, outlines, and effects to shapes, and how to add text to a shape to give your message more punch. You'll also learn how to edit a shape or create your own for those special messages that need a little more zing.

When to Use Shapes

In Chapter 1, you learned that "less is more." This is an important design concept that will serve you well as you create your PowerPoint 2007 slides. The main thing to remember is that one stunning element can make an extraordinary statement in the midst of messages on top of messages that are vying for attention. Using shapes as well as other options sparingly are your best bet for creating dramatic, memorable slides.

Take a moment to determine your message. What are you trying to communicate? Are you trying to make your audience laugh, or are you conveying a poignant moment? Are you closing the deal with your most important selling points, or are you providing a high-level overview of the product's benefits? Determining what you want to communicate will be the first step in selecting the shape you'll use.

Selecting and Inserting a Shape

You'll find the Shapes command on the Insert tab:

1. Go to the Insert tab.

2. From the Illustrations group, select Shapes.

3. From the Shapes options, shown to the left, select the shape you prefer.

4. Size and position the shape on the slide.

The Drawing Tools Format Tab

The Drawing Tools Format tab is where you'll find most of the commands you need to take advantage of all that Shapes has to offer. Highlight the shape and then click the Drawing Tools Format tab to see the complete toolbar. This toolbar has the same groups and commands as WordArt, which is described in Chapter 7.

Adding Fill to a Shape

Once you're on the Drawing Tools Format tab, you have two ways to add fill to a shape from the Shape Styles group. You can use the Shape Fill command

THE WHITE SPACE THAT SHAPES YOUR WORLD

Shapes help us define our world. One of our first exercises in early childhood was fitting the round piece of the puzzle into the round hole, the square piece into the square hole, and so on.

Artists are shape experts because they see the world with a perspective that's a little different than the rest of us. When they draw, they don't simply draw the shape's actual lines and curves. They focus on the shape's lines, curves, shadows, and white space.

For instance, when an artist draws a face, she looks at the points where the light falls. Most portraits do

not use actual lines to define features like the lips, nose, and eyes. If you look closely, however, you'll see the artist used shadows and white space to create a representation of these features.

Take a moment to think about everyday shapes you see. Look around while you're walking in your neighborhood or sitting outside. You'll probably be surprised at the amount of white space and shadows contained in each shape. Use this knowledge as you create your shapes in PowerPoint 2007, and you can design 3D effects that come alive on the slide.

or choose an option from the Shape Styles Gallery. Let's take a look at both methods.

1. Go to the Shape Styles group.

2. Click Shape Fill.

3. Roll your cursor over the colors for a Live Preview.

4. Select the color you prefer.

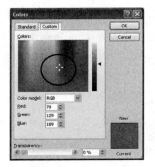

If you don't like the colors in the Theme Colors section, you can find additional colors or create your own custom color. Click More Fill Colors and then select the Standard tab and choose a color. To the right of the color palette, you'll see the color you selected at the top of the square under New, while the Current color is shown below it. You can adjust the Transparency setting for the color at the bottom of the dialog box by entering a percentage number or by dragging the scroll bar to the right.

110

THE EASY WAY

See a color you like in the Custom tab and just want to get to it quickly? Look for the white cursor, as shown above in the Custom color palette. Simply drag the cursor to the color you want and then release the mouse button. Click OK. This will help you enhance the shapes in your presentation with varying shades of color more quickly.

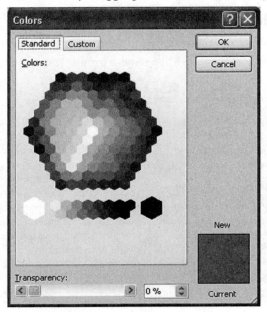

Not sure what color you want, but want to experiment a bit? Click More Fill Colors and then select the Custom tab. Here, you'll see RGB (Red, Green, Blue) colors that you can adjust by dragging the arrow to the right of the vertical bar or by adjusting the amount of each color in the Red, Green, Blue fields below the palette.

If you'd prefer a different color palette, in the Color Model drop-down list, select

MEMO

When you use the Custom tab in the Colors dialog box, write down the numbers in the RGB or HSL fields and keep them in a convenient place. This will save time when you want to use the color again but don't want to search for it in a previously created shape. You can also find it listed as a Recent Color in the drop-down box from either the Shape Fill, Shape Outline, or Font Color commands.

HSL (Hue, Saturation, Luminosity). Adjust the colors by dragging the arrow to the right of the vertical bar or by adjusting the amounts in the fields below the palette.

PowerPoint 2007 has a number of attractive textures that make for a great-looking fill for your shape. From material to marble to wood to swimming fish, the Texture command gives you plenty of options to make your shape come alive on your slide.

1. Click the Shape Fill command.

2. Select Texture.

3. Select a texture you like.

Figure 8-1 uses the Woven Mat texture, whereas Figure 8-2 uses the White Marble texture and Figure 8-3 uses the Oak texture. Take time to explore the textures in PowerPoint 2007 to see how they can work in your presentation, or add a texture from a file or clip art.

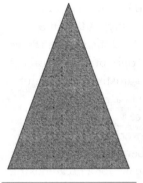

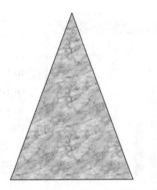

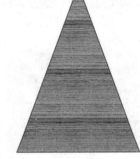

Figure 8-1   The Woven Mat texture

Figure 8-2   The White Marble texture

Figure 8-3   The Oak texture

Adding an Outline to a Shape

As you learned in the previous chapter on WordArt, adding an outline to an object can make a big difference in engaging your audience quickly. The steps to adding an outline to a shape are similar to that of WordArt. From the Drawing Tools Format tab, click Shape Outline and then select a color for your outline. From here, you can adjust the weight of the line and choose whether you want to use a solid or dashed line for your outline.

Adding Shape Effects

Using Shape Effects can bring a little excitement to your presentation. You can use these effects to create an ethereal feeling with a subtle glow or add some depth with the Bevel effect. Adding a reflection and softening the edges are other options to help you create the mood for your slide. Let's look at quickly changing a shape by adding some color and depth:

1. Click the Shapes command and then select the round diagonal corner rectangle from the Rectangles section.

2. Click the Shape Fill command, and then select Orange, Accent 6, Lighter 80%.

Link   *30,000 Years of Art*, by the Editors of Phaidon, Phaidon Press Inc., 2007.

Figure 8-4   The Bevel effect

3. Click the Shape Outline command, and then select Red, Accent 2.

4. Select the Shape Outline command again, and then select Weight and click 6 point.

5. Click the Shape Effects command and then Bevel.

6. Choose Riblet.

Using the Bevel effect in Figure 8-4 adds dimension to your shape.

Adding Text to a Shape

Using shapes with text can really target what you're saying with a captivating visual mix of words and shapes. Let's use a number of commands to create a shape with text:

1. Select the Shapes command, and select the right arrow in the Block Arrows section.

2. Click the Shape Fill command, and select Green from the Standard Colors tab.

3. Click the Shape Outline command, and select Yellow from the Standard Colors tab.

4. Click the Shape Outline command again, and select Weight and click 6 point.

5. Click the Shape Outline command, and select Dashes and then Square Dot.

6. Click the Shape Effects command, and then select Shadow and Perspective Diagonal Upper Left from the Perspective section.

113

You can add text to a shape in two ways. One way is from the Insert Shapes group. Select Text Box to add text to your shape.

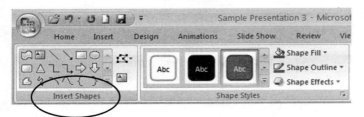

You can also add WordArt to your shape. From the WordArt Styles group, select Quick Styles and select the Word-Art style you like.

Let's add some WordArt to the shape you just created.

1. Using the Quick Styles command in the WordArt Styles group, select Fill-White, Drop Shadow.

2. Highlight and increase the text point size to 96.

3. In the popup that appears when the WordArt is highlighted, select Italicize.

4. Go to the Text Outline command and change the color to Yellow.

5. Go to Text Effects and select Glow.

6. Click More Glow Colors.

7. Select Dark Blue, Text 2.

Figure 8-5 shows many layers and effects for the shape as well as the WordArt.

Editing and Sizing Shapes

Occasionally, you'll need a particular shape for a certain situation. PowerPoint 2007 gives you options for editing and changing the ready-made shapes as needed. You can also create your own shapes from scratch. We'll explore both options so you'll have more versatility in PowerPoint 2007.

Figure 8-5   Adding WordArt to a shape

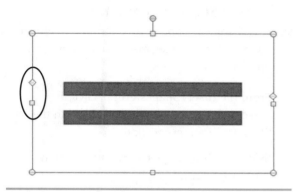

Figure 8-6   Editing a shape with the left yellow marker

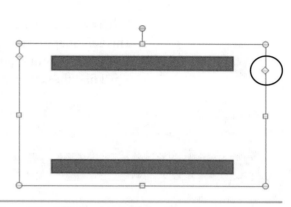

Figure 8-7   Editing a shape with the right yellow marker

Editing Ready-Made Shapes with Markers

Go to the Insert tab. Select Shapes | Equation Shapes and select the equal sign. When the shape is highlighted, you'll see two yellow diamonds on each vertical line of the Shape box.

Put your cursor on the yellow diamond marker on the left and drag it down a bit. Notice in Figure 8-6 how this makes the lines thinner.

Now drag the yellow marker on the right vertical line up a bit. In Figure 8-7, notice how the lines are farther apart.

Anytime your shape has the yellow markers, you can adjust the shape in any way you like. Let's look at another shape we can adjust. On a new slide, go to the Insert tab. Then select Shapes | Block Arrows. Choose the left-right arrow. Drag the yellow marker on the right down. Drag the left yellow marker to the left. Figure 8-8 displays a ready-made arrow adjusted for specific shape needs.

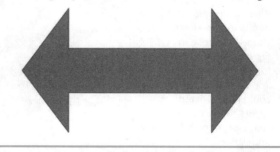

Figure 8-8   A ready-made shape edited with yellow markers

115

Editing a Shape from the Edit Shape Command

The Edit Shape command lets you change a shape or turn it into a freeform shape. A freeform shape has curved and straight segments you can adjust. You'll find the command in the Insert Shapes group.

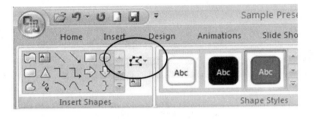

1. From the Insert Shapes group, click the Explosion 2 shape, the second shape in the Stars And Banners section.

2. Select the Edit Shape command and then Convert To Freeform.

3. Select the Edit Shape command again.

4. Click Edit Points.

In Figure 8-9, you see a number of points on the shape. From here, you can adjust the shape by dragging the points where you like. Figure 8-10 shows how a freeform shape can be reshaped and resized by dragging a few of the points.

To change a shape from the Edit Shape command, simply click the shape and select Edit Shape | Change Shape and select the new shape.

Use the Reroute Connectors command when you have a flow chart or diagram where two or more connector lines connect the same two objects. This command moves all the lines so they connect at the same points in the most direct way. If you want to reroute only one line, select the line before clicking Reroute Connectors.

MEMO

When dragging points in a freeform shape like those in Figure 8-9, be careful to pull in a straight line or your shape could have twisted points that make the shape uneven and unbalanced.

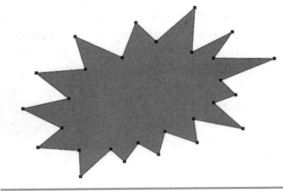

Figure 8-9   Editing points in a freeform shape

Figure 8-10   An edited freeform shape

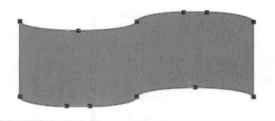

Figure 8-11   Edit points in the freeform shape

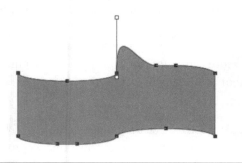

Figure 8-12   The white point markers let you create new parts of the shape while keeping the edit points in their original locations.

Let's experiment with another ready-made shape by converting it to a freeform shape. From the Insert Shapes group, select Shapes and then Flowchart: Punched Tape from the Flowchart section. Go to the Drawing Tools Format tab. Click Edit Shape | Convert To Freeform | Edit Points. In Figure 8-11, you'll see the point pattern to use to create a new form.

Let's drag some of these points to see what we can create. When you click a point, you'll see two white markers next to the point. These markers help you create or move part of the shape while keeping the original shape points in place, as you see in Figure 8-12.

Creating a Shape from the Freeform or Scribble Commands

In PowerPoint 2007, you can also create your own shapes from the Home tab. As we mentioned earlier, a freeform shape has curved and straight segments, whereas the Scribble command lets you create smooth curves or gives your shapes the look of being drawn by hand with a pen. We're sure you'll find plenty of uses for both of these commands once you start using shapes in your presentations.

1.   Go to the Home tab.

2.   Click Shapes.

3.   From the Lines section, select Freeform.

4.   Create your shape anywhere on your slide.

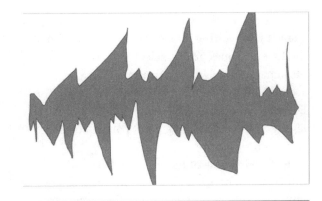

Figure 8-13   A freeform shape

Figure 8-14   The Scribble command

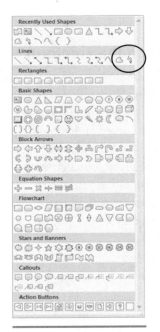

5.   Double-click to finish the shape, or to close the shape, click near your starting point.

Figure 8-13 is an example of a freeform shape. In Figure 8-14, you'll see an example of what you can do with the Scribble command. You can use this command to sign your name or create a shape with curves. You'll find this command next to Freeform in the Lines section of Shapes, as shown in Figure 8-15.

Click Scribble. And then begin writing or drawing anywhere on the page. When you're finished, double-click.

Working with the Freeform and Scribble commands will take some practice, but once you become more confident, you'll be a pro at designing shapes, signatures, and just about anything you can think of. A couple of helpful hints for both of these features:

- To see the details better, set Zoom to 200 or 400 percent. This way, you'll be sure to see every nuance of your shape. You'll find Zoom on the View tab.

Figure 8-15   Selecting freeform and scribble lines

MEMO

Using the Scribble command well requires a little practice, especially if you're using it for a signature or general handwriting. Take some time to get used to the sensitivity of your mouse and how much pressure and movement it takes to create handwriting that's legible. You may want to start small and then begin to make your movements bigger as you become more proficient using this command.

■ From the Control Panel, reset your point to the slowest speed available. This helps significantly with control as you learn how to create shapes from scratch.

In this chapter, you learned about a number of ways to use shapes in a dynamic presentation. In addition to using shape fill, outline, effects, and text, you also learned how to edit a ready-made shape and how to create your own shape.

119

Comparing and Illustrating Content with SmartArt

If you haven't really used SmartArt yet, you're going to be quite impressed by what it can do. If you have used it, then you know that it can make life substantially easier when designing a presentation. The beauty of *SmartArt*—a visual method for displaying your content—is that it turns simple text into dynamic graphics that are easy to read and understand. In particular, SmartArt lets you show concepts, processes, hierarchies, and other relationships in a visual way by providing preset graphics that you can simply drop your information into. You can customize both the look and layout of SmartArt and animate it as well.

We'll also show you how to work with charts, which are wonderful graphic elements that you can add to presentations in which you need to display numerical data. Charts aren't quite as flexible as SmartArt, but you can still make them look professional using color and the Quick Styles Gallery.

In this chapter, we'll explain what SmartArt and charts entail and how they both work. You'll learn how to edit SmartArt, instantly change basic text into SmartArt, and perform a range of other tasks to make your SmartArt the coolest in town. Plus, you'll discover how to change chart elements easily and apply a variety of elements to your charts to make them stand out from a graphic perspective.

SmartArt Overview

SmartArt offers more than 80 different graphic layouts and can be used in PowerPoint 2007, Word 2007, and Excel 2007. These 80 layouts are separated into seven groups:

- **List** Use to display grouped, related, or even nonsequential information.

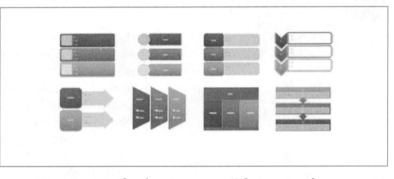

- **Process** Use for showing sequential steps or subgroups.

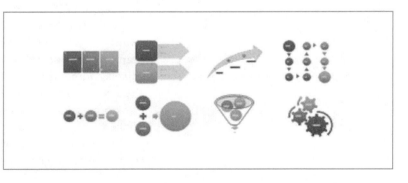

■ **Cycle**   Use to show a continuing sequence of stages or relationships to a central idea.

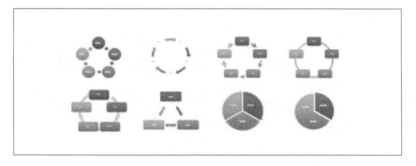

■ **Hierarchy**   Use to display groups of information and reporting relationships.

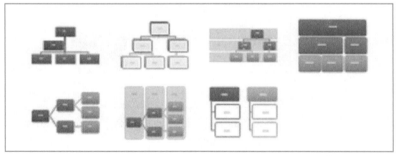

SMARTART VS. CHARTS

You might think SmartArt simply duplicates the Chart function in PowerPoint, but these are truly two different types of tools. Whereas SmartArt helps you display information and ideas in a visual manner, charts help you illustrate numeric values or data. If you're trying to decide between the two, take a good look at the content you need to display. If it's text-based, you're probably better off with SmartArt. If it involves a lot of numbers, go with the Chart function.

■ **Relationship**   Use to display information that overlaps or is somehow interrelated. This option is particularly good for showing comparisons.

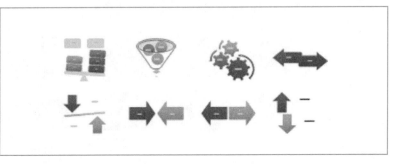

■ **Matrix**   Use to show relationships of components to a whole.

■ **Pyramid**   Use to display proportional, interconnected, or hierarchical relationships.

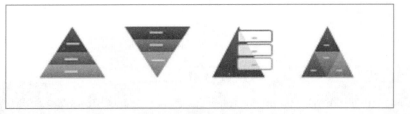

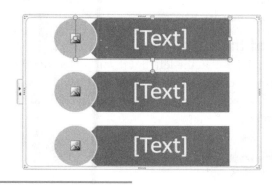

Figure 9-1   SmartArt list graphic—Vertical Picture Accent List

The SmartArt Tabs

To get started, you'll need to insert a SmartArt shape into a presentation. For example purposes, go to Insert | Illustrations | SmartArt and select Vertical Picture Accent List. Click OK. Your graphic should look like the one shown in Figure 9-1.

Now, with the SmartArt selected, you will see two new tabs in the Ribbon: SmartArt Tools Design and SmartArt Tools Format. If it's not already selected, choose the SmartArt Tools Design tab.

SmartArt Tools Design Tab

This tab, shown in Figure 9-2, is where you'll do most of your graphic work on a piece of SmartArt. With it, you can make a variety of instant layout changes, work with text, add shapes, and change colors.

125

![SmartArt Tools Design tab ribbon]

Figure 9-2   The SmartArt Tools Design tab

Viewing from left to right, you'll see that the tab has four command groups: Create Graphic, Layouts, SmartArt Styles, and Reset. We'll explain the functions in each of these so you see how easily you can manipulate your SmartArt layout.

Add Shapes to the Layout

In the SmartArt example on your slide, you'll see six primary shapes: three circles on the left side and three horizontal boxes on the right side. This combination gives you *three* basic SmartArt shapes. But let's assume you need a total of five basic shapes. To add an additional shape below the first three, select the bottom shape and select Create Graphic | Add Shape | Add Shape After. Add the fifth shape using The Easy Way.

Change the Direction of the Layout

In the previous example the circles are on the left, but if you prefer that they be located on the right, you can quickly swap the shapes, as shown below. In the SmartArt Tools Design tab, select Create Graphic | Right To Left and the SmartArt will instantly be reversed.

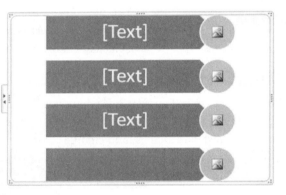

Add Text to the Layout

Click on the top shape where it says [*Text*], and type **The cow jumped over the moon.** You'll notice how the text wraps automatically to fit the shape; if you want to change how the text looks within the shape, simply right-click and select Format Shape | Text Box. To learn more about using the specific Text Box functions available in the Format Shape dialog box, see Chapter 8.

You can also add text to the layout by selecting Text Pane in the Create Graphic command group. Some people prefer using the Text pane because it allows them to work with text and bullets more easily; others simply prefer to type within the graphic itself. Whether you use the Text pane (shown in

MEMO

You can open the Text pane by clicking the double-arrow handle on the side of your SmartArt, too. To close it, click Close in the Text pane or click Text Pane again in the Create Graphic command group.

Figure 9-3) or type in the graphic itself, as soon as you add a second bullet or a second shape and begin to type, the Promote and/or Demote commands will become active in the Create Graphic command group.

With these commands, you can instantly move text to another shape. For example, if you type **The moon jumped over the cow** next to the second bullet, the Demote command becomes active. Click it and **The moon jumped over the cow** instantly becomes a subbullet under **The cow jumped over the moon.** You can move it back to the second shape by selecting Promote, which is now active.

Type your text here   ✕

- The cow jumped over the moon.
- The moon jumped over the cow.
- [Text]
-

Vertical Picture Accent List...

Figure 9-3   The Text pane

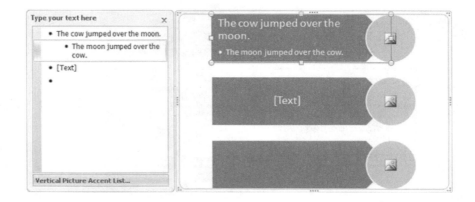

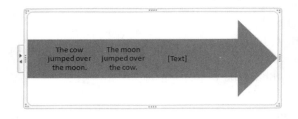

Figure 9-4 Selecting a new layout is easy, and all your text will transfer as well.

Change the Layout Midstream

If you get into your design and realize that the SmartArt graphic you've chosen simply isn't working, don't fret. Go to the Layouts command group, and click the More arrow to see all the layouts from the group type you originally selected. Hover your mouse over the layouts in the Gallery to see whether any other shapes work; if not, select More Layouts to return to the original Choose A SmartArt Graphic dialog box.

You won't be able to see a Live Preview of the choices, but you'll have the entire list of layouts at your disposal. Click one to change your SmartArt instantly. In Figure 9-4, we changed the layout from the original horizontal box and circle to an arrow using this process.

For purposes of this continuing example, we'll change back to the original SmartArt graphic, however.

Change Colors Throughout the Layout

SmartArt layout colors are based on the theme you have applied to your presentation, but you can easily change them. Click Change Colors in the SmartArt Styles command group. A menu of colors will appear; simply select a new color grouping from that menu. In the menu, the current color option will be highlighted for you. Later in this chapter, we'll show you how to change individual shape colors within your SmartArt graphic.

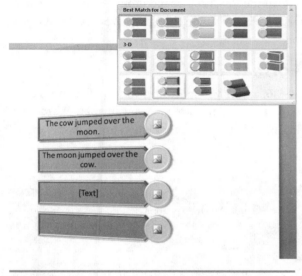

Apply SmartArt Styles

Just like in other areas of PowerPoint, you can apply preset styles to SmartArt. Click the More arrow next to the Gallery in the SmartArt Styles command group to see the options for the piece of SmartArt you've chosen. In Figure 9-5, we selected Metallic Scene from the Gallery.

Add a Picture to Your SmartArt

In the example we've been using throughout this chapter, you've probably noticed the picture icon (shown here) in the center of the circle shape. This icon means that you can easily place a photograph in the shape. Simply click the icon, and the Insert Picture dialog box will appear. Select the picture you want to use from your hard drive, and click Insert. The picture will be placed into your SmartArt in the form of the shape where the icon was located. In this case, the photos are formatted into circle shapes. Later in this chapter, we'll show you how to insert a photo into a shape that does not contain the picture icon.

Figure 9-5   Apply a SmartArt Style from the Gallery to change the look of your SmartArt graphic immediately.

129

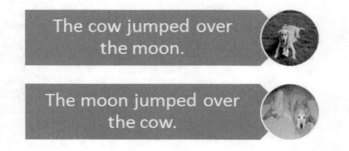

Reset the SmartArt Graphic

If you've changed the SmartArt and then decide you don't like any of the changes, select Reset Graphic in the Reset command group. Be careful when you use this option; it will remove every single change you've made to the graphic except text additions.

SmartArt Tools Format Tab

This tab, as shown in Figure 9-6, allows you to make a variety of changes to SmartArt text and shapes in particular. For example, you can apply WordArt to your SmartArt using this tab, and you can change the color or nature of your shapes.

WHICH TYPES OF LEARNERS ARE IN YOUR AUDIENCE?

Every person learns differently. Some prefer to read information to absorb it, whereas others want to see the action in a visual format to retain it. In fact, seven primary learning-style types have been identified:

- **Visual** Prefers learning with images, pictures, colors, and maps. SmartArt, relevant pictures, and other graphics work well for these people.

- **Aural** Learns most easily by working with sounds and music. Using sounds in your presentation can capture this person's attention.

- **Verbal** Learns equally well with both written and spoken words. This person will do fine with bulleted text and nothing else on the slide.

- **Physical** Learns best when using the body or sense of touch to explore concepts. These people are the ones who can't sit still during your presentation!

- **Logical** Understands patterns, numbers, and connections well. These people tend to like charts and SmartArt.

- **Social** Learns by bouncing ideas off other people and by working in groups. This person might come up to you after the presentation to make comments or ask for more information.

- **Solitary** Learns through independent thought and deep analysis, which makes this person a tough sell using a group presentation. A solution is to offer this person the presentation to review on his own so he can review it at his leisure.

When you present to an audience, no matter how small, remember that all types of learners might be present. Use a combination of graphics, animations, text, and sound to highlight key points; just be sure not to overwhelm your audience by placing all these items on the same slide!

Figure 9-6   The SmartArt
Tools Format tab

Viewing from left to right, you'll see that the tab has five command
groups: Shapes, Shape Styles, WordArt Styles, Arrange, and Size. Since
WordArt Styles are covered in Chapter 7 and Shape Styles are covered in
Chapter 8, this chapter will focus only briefly on those two command groups.
In this chapter, we'll primarily cover the Shapes group to show you how
applying Shape and WordArt styles can make your SmartArt truly pop for
your audience.

Edit 3D SmartArt in 2D

When you select a 3D style for your SmartArt, working in it can be a little
confusing when you're trying to edit the shape. Click Edit In 2-D in the
Shapes command group to revert the SmartArt to a flat graphic that's easier
to work with; then click that command again to return to 3D mode.

Change the Look of an Individual Shape Within SmartArt

Perhaps you like the general look of your SmartArt, but you'd like to change
the format of one or more of the shapes within the graphic. No problem. Just
follow these steps:

1.   Select the shape that you want to change in the graphic.

2.   Click Change Shape in the Shapes command group.

3.   Select the new shape you want to apply.

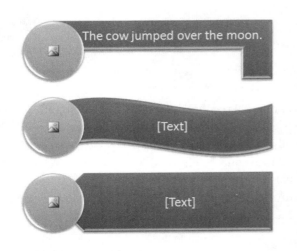

In Figure 9-7, we changed the top horizontal shape to look like a horizontal *L* using the L-Shape and the middle shape to a wave using the Wave shape; we left the bottom shape alone.

Apply a Style to an Individual Shape Within SmartArt

Shape Styles were explored in detail in Chapter 8, but we'll cover them again briefly to show you how they can be used inside a piece of SmartArt. Using the SmartArt from Figure 9-7, we applied different Shape Styles to each shape within the graphic to demonstrate how you can play with shape styles to achieve a completely unique look for your SmartArt. If you're attempting to use SmartArt to draw attention to various elements of a topic, this method can help you differentiate among elements even as the entire graphic shows the whole.

To apply a new style to a shape within a SmartArt graphic, just follow these steps:

Figure 9-7 You can change individual shapes within a piece of Smart Art.

1. Select the shape that you want to change in the graphic.

2. Click More in the Shape Styles command group.

3. Click the new style you want to apply.

As you can see in Figure 9-8, the graphic now looks totally different from Figure 9-7. It still retains the custom shapes, however. The table shown next reveals how we did it using the Shape Styles Gallery.

MEMO

Don't forget, when you outline an object you can not only change the color of the outline but also the weight and look of it, too. Use the Weight and Dashes commands to make these changes.

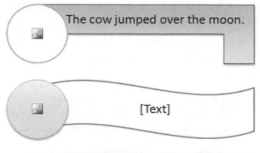

Figure 9-8   SmartArt can be manipulated shape by shape by applying Shape Styles to individual shapes.

133

Shape	Options
Top circle	Colored Outline, Accent 6
Top horizontal L	Subtle Effect, Dark 1
Center circle	Subtle Effect, Accent 5
Middle wave	Colored Outline, Accent 5
Bottom circle	Intense Effect, Accent 5
Bottom horizontal box	Colored Fill, Accent 6

Change Colors and Borders of Individual Shapes

Earlier we explained how to change colors throughout a piece of SmartArt. Here, we'll show you how to change colors and borders within individual shapes. The command to change shape colors is located in the Shape Styles command group; select the shape where you want to change the color and then click Shape Fill and choose a new color.

You can change the shape outline or *border* just as easily using the Shape Outline command in this same group. Select the shape where you want to change the border and then click Shape Outline and choose a new outline.

Add a Picture to a Shape Without a Picture Icon

When a picture icon appears in SmartArt, it indicates that the shape can accept and automatically resize a picture to fit the specific shape involved. Your pictures don't get too terribly distorted this way. However, you can still add pictures to other shapes if you like. Just be aware that they might be stretched a little oddly or otherwise look a tad goofy. You can always undo the command if you don't like how the picture looks, so give it a try by following these steps in any SmartArt shape that does not have a picture icon within it:

1. Select the shape.
2. Go to Shape Fill in the Shape Styles group.
3. Click Picture.
4. Select a picture and click Insert.

The picture will be inserted into your graphic as shown in Figure 9-9. In the example, you can see how the photos are stretched; you can play with the shape's size to see if that helps the photo look more normal.

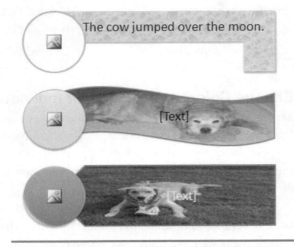

Figure 9-9   Photos can be added to any shape in SmartArt.

Convert Slide Text to SmartArt Instantly

You don't have to start out with SmartArt as you build your slide; you can begin with text and then quickly convert that text to SmartArt if you prefer. Although the process works most effectively with bulleted text, you can make the conversion even with just one word or sentence. Here's how to do it:

1. Type text on a slide.

2. Right-click the text box.

3. Select Convert To SmartArt.

4. Select a SmartArt shape.

Your text will now appear as the SmartArt option you chose.

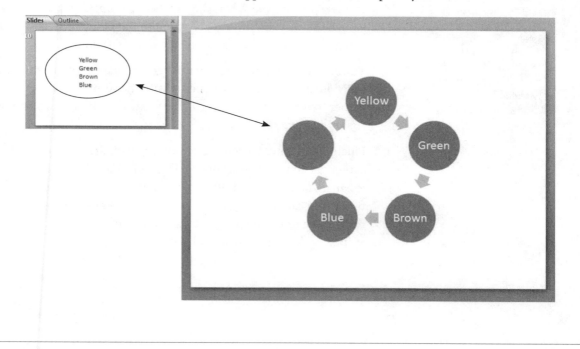

MEMO

Connecting lines connect two shapes and stay connected to those shapes. They will have connection points at each end and appear as red dots. The dots show you where you can attach a connecting line to a shape. You can reroute connecting lines to make more direct connections if you wish. To do that, go to the Drawing Tools Format tab and the Insert Shapes command group. Select | Edit Shape | Reroute Connectors or you can manually move the connectors as needed.

Animating with SmartArt

All right, so now we get to the true fun of SmartArt: animation. Although we'll explain animation in more detail in Chapter 12, we'll show you a few things you can do with SmartArt right now. You can animate SmartArt just like you would animate almost any other object, but here are a few caveats:

- First, the order in which the shapes appear in your SmartArt will dictate the order in which the animation plays. You can't pick and choose which shapes will animate at a particular time, although you can, of course, reverse your entire SmartArt graphic to animate it in reverse if you like.

- Second, treat each SmartArt graphic as the unique item it is. Animations will occur in different ways given the type of SmartArt involved, so we can't possibly explain all the different combinations in a few paragraphs. When you first begin animating SmartArt, allow yourself some extra time to play around. But don't try to figure it all out when you've got a heavy deadline for your presentation.

- Third, connecting lines between SmartArt shapes will not animate individually—they always associate with the second shape. Don't bother trying to change it; you'll just waste a lot of precious time on something that can't be done.

- Finally, use caution when you're working with diagrams created in earlier versions of PowerPoint. If those diagrams have been converted to SmartArt and animation is applied, the animation might get pretty funky. You can try—it does work sometimes—but if you start having trouble, we recommend just starting over from scratch or ditching the animation for that particular object.

To animate your entire piece of SmartArt, follow these steps:

1. Select the SmartArt graphic.

2. Go to the Animations tab.

3. In the Animations group, click the arrow to the right of Animate. Text may appear in the box beside Animate that says No Animation or you might see other animation effect text.

4. Select an animation effect from the options provided in the menu.

137

THE EASY WAY

If you want to show the shapes one by one, choose a One By One option under Fade, Wipe, or Fly In from the Animate menu. Then click Custom Animation to open the Custom Animation pane on your screen. Select On Click in the Start box. This method will make every object in your SmartArt appear consecutively but only as you click the mouse.

This chapter explored how to use SmartArt in your presentations. As you can see, PowerPoint offers lots of graphic possibilities and probably thousands of ways to manipulate your SmartArt for unique, professional graphics. Coming up in the next chapter, you'll learn how to drop movies into your presentation.

Adding a Movie to Your Presentation

Movies in PowerPoint 2007 can really spice up your presentation. With all the technology available to us today, why not use it to your advantage? This chapter on movies, along with the next chapter on sound, will keep all eyes—and ears—on your presentation. The more ways you present the information, the better the chance your audience will comprehend and remember it.

How Movies Can Benefit a Presentation

If you've been anywhere on the Internet, you'll know that movies have become commonplace in our lives. Type video clips into your search engine and you'll get an amazing array of results. You can easily see how people use videos to make others laugh or cry or think. Even if only motivated to find their fame and fortune through venues like YouTube, today's population is comfortable watching movies in a variety of venues beyond the movie theater.

Adding movies to your presentation may not help you achieve your own fame and fortune, but it can mean you've got your audience's undivided attention in a world where messages are consistently coming at us. Including a movie in your presentation means you've taken your presentation to the next level—the entertainment level. And let's face it: All audiences want to be entertained. So if you can add some pizzazz with a movie, go for it!

Again, we remind you about what you learned in Chapter 1: Less is more. Focus your movie in an area where you really want to highlight a specific idea or storyline. Don't add movies just because they're fun—even though they are! Add movies to make your point in a stronger, more inviting way.

Supported Movie File Formats

Before we get to movie specifics, let's look at the movie file formats supported by PowerPoint 2007. You can insert these file formats into your presentation:

- Windows Media file (.asf)
- Windows Video file (.avi)
- Movie file (.mpg or .mpeg)
- Windows Media Video file (.wmv)

If your movie is not in one of these formats, it will not play in PowerPoint 2007. However, you can convert it to one of these formats using a utility, program, or add-in. Try one of these:

- **Microsoft Windows Media Encoder**   A free program that makes some files compatible with PowerPoint 2007. Visit http://www.microsoft .com/windows/windowsmedia/forpros/encoder/default.mspx for more information.

- **PFCMedia**   An add-in that automates the formatting of multimedia. For more information, visit PFCMedia for PowerPoint at http://office .microsoft.com/en-us/marketplace/EM012132961033.aspx.

Inserting a Movie from a File

PowerPoint 2007 makes it easy to insert a movie that is in the correct file format.

1.   Go to the Insert tab.

2.   In the Media Clip group, select Movie.

HOW MOVIES WORK WITHIN YOUR PRESENTATION

An important item to remember when you're inserting movies into PowerPoint 2007: Movies are *linked* to your presentation; they are *not embedded* into the presentation itself. This means that you should always copy your movies into the same folder as your presentation so PowerPoint 2007 can link to and find them easily. Even if you move the folder to another computer, you'll still have your movies and presentation together. If you have problems running your movie, your first step will be to confirm that both of these items are in the same folder.

One easy way to make sure all the items are in one folder is to use the Package For CD option. Click Microsoft Office | Publish | Package For CD. From here, you can copy to a folder or CD, and when you click Options, you can choose how to package the presentation, whether to include linked files (which you'll always want to do when running a movie) or embedded TrueType fonts, and whether to include a password in order to run the presentation.

3. Click Movie From File.

4. Select the movie you want to insert into the presentation.

5. Click OK.

You can also double-click the movie file to insert it into your presentation. You'll see a Microsoft Office PowerPoint dialog box that asks when you would like to have the movie play. Your options are

- **Automatically**   This option means your movie plays when the slide displays. If you're using other media effects like animation, the movie will play after the animation. You can pause the movie by clicking it; restart it by clicking it again.

- **When Clicked**   This option means your movie will play when you click it. This is also known as a *trigger*.

- **Play Across Slides**   This option plays the movie for the length of the movie file one time. It does not play the movie more than once. (To play the movie continuously, check the Loop Until Stopped checkbox in the Movie Options group.)

THE EASY WAY

Want to be sure your movie plays for the entire presentation? From the Animations group, select Custom Animations. In the Play Movie dialog box, enter the number 999 in the After field. This number generally appears as the default and is the maximum number you can enter. By doing this, you won't have to adjust the value if you add or delete slides in the presentation.

You can make changes to these options later, depending on how you want the movie to play. If you select the Play Across Slides option, you'll need to go to the Animations tab. From the Animations tab, go to the Animations group and select Custom Animation | Custom Animation Pane. Click the line with the triangle, and then click the down arrow and choose Effect Options. You'll then see the Play Movie dialog box.

On the Effect tab, go to the Stop section and click After and enter the total number of slides you want the movie to play across.

Once you've inserted your movie, you'll see a new toolbar in the Movie Tools Options tab. Let's go through each of the groups and commands on this toolbar.

In the Play group, you can Preview your movie. Click the Preview icon now to see your movie in PowerPoint 2007.

The Movie Options group has a number of commands, including:

- **Slide Show Volume**   From this command, you can adjust the volume of your movie or mute the sound altogether. The default volume is Medium.

- **Play Movie**   This command lets you select whether to play the movie automatically, which we selected earlier, to play when clicked, or to play across the slides.

- **Hide During Show**   Check this box to hide the sound or movie icon during the slide show.

- **Play Full Screen**   Use this command for the movie to play on the entire screen.

- **Loop Until Stopped**   This command sets up the sound or movie to continue playing until manually stopped.

- **Rewind Movie After Playing**   This command automatically rewinds the movie back to the first frame once it's finished playing.

You can also access these options by clicking the arrow in the bottom-right corner of the Movie Options group. You'll see the Movie Options dialog box that lets you adjust your movie according to your needs, along with checking the total movie playing time.

We'll explore the Arrange group commands later in this chapter, but let's take a brief look at the Size group. As you learned in Chapter 3, the Size group lets you change the size of your picture or movie on the slide. You can make changes directly in the Size group, or if you click the arrow in the bottom-right corner of the group, you'll see the Size And Position dialog box. The Size tab in this dialog box lets you size, scale, crop, or reset your picture to its original size. The Position tab lets you select where you want the picture on the slide.

Inserting a Clip Art Movie

You can also insert a clip art movie, which is actually an animated GIF file and not really a movie. Instead, the file is a number of images that stream to create an animated effect.

1. Go to the Insert tab.

2. In the Media Clip group, select Movie.

3. Click Movie From Clip Art Pane.

The Clip Art pane will appear. This pane will be similar to the one you learned about in Chapter 5, but you'll be reviewing animated GIFs instead of still clip art. (This is because you inserted a Movie From Clip Organizer instead of the Clip Art command in the Illustrations group.)

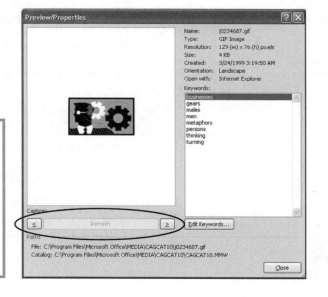

In the Clip Art pane, hover your cursor above the yellow star in the bottom-right corner of one of the frames. Then click the down arrow, shown here, and Preview/Properties.

The Preview/Properties dialog box gives you a preview of the clip art movie. Notice how some are larger and some are smaller? As a rule, you can generally make a large animated GIF smaller and maintain the same effect, but making smaller GIFs larger generally means you'll lose the picture and/or the animation effects.

We encourage you to play a bit now. Select a few GIFs of varying sizes, resize them as you like, and then go to the Slide Show tab. From the Start Slide Show group, select From Beginning to see how they look.

145

THE EASY WAY

Want to review all the animated GIFs in the Clip Art pane quickly? In the Preview/Properties dialog box, click the right arrow in the scroll bar below the GIF preview. You can review all the animated GIFs in the order they appear in the pane, without clicking each individual GIF. To review a GIF you've already seen, simply click the left arrow to go back. Or, if you only want a specific topic, type it into the Search field at the top of the pane and click Go.

Arranging Movies and Clip Art on the Slide

Once inserted, you can arrange movies and animated clip art anywhere on the slide by simply dragging them where you like. Let's try this now.

1. Go to the Insert tab.

2. In the Media Clip group, select Movie.

3. Click Movie From File.

4. Select the movie you want to insert into the presentation.

5. From the Insert tab in the Media Clip group, select Movie.

6. Click Movie From Clip Organizer.

7. Select the animated GIF you want to insert.

8. From the Insert tab in the Text group, click Text Box.

9. Place your cursor on the slide and type a message.

10. Arrange the objects on the slide as you like.

When you insert the animated clip art, it will appear on top of your movie. You can arrange the GIF, movie, and text box as you like, resizing boxes and text as needed. If you need to align the objects, go to the Movie Tools Options tab, and select Arrange | Align | View Gridlines. Now you can see the gridlines to help you line up objects, as shown in Figure 10-1. We dragged our movie down the slide, added and sized text, and inserted two animated GIFs (j0283572.gif) from the Clip Organizer. When viewing this slide in Slide Show mode, you'll see the two butterflies at the top fluttering their wings as the movie runs. When the movie is finished, the GIFs continue to flutter until you click to move to the next page.

Now, let's see how you can use a picture as a background to highlight your movie when it plays.

Figure 10-1 A movie, two animated GIFs, and text box aligned using gridlines

1. From the Home tab, go to the Slides group.

2. Click New Slide and select Blank.

3. From the Insert tab in the Illustrations group, click Picture.

4. Select a photo to use for the background of your slide.

5. Go to the Picture Tools Format tab.

6. In the Adjust group, click Recolor and select Grayscale in the Color Modes section.

7. In the Adjust group, click Brightness and select +40%.

8. In the Adjust group, click Contrast and select −40%.

9. Go to the Picture Styles group and click Picture Border.

10. Click Black, Text 1.

11. Click Picture Border and select Weight.

12. Select 3 point.

Now you've created a grayscale background for your movie to run on. Go to the Insert tab, and in Media Clip group, select Movie | Movie From File. Select the movie you want to insert into the presentation. You should have a slide that looks similar to Figure 10-2. Adding the background gives some depth and interest to your slide.

Figure 10-2 A movie running on a grayscale background

147

Performance Considerations

When using movies in a PowerPoint 2007 presentation, remember that too much activity on a slide can delay or completely halt the movie's ability to play. And using a number of movies or animated clip art items can increase your file size significantly, which could lead to performance issues as well. To improve your presentation's performance:

1. Go to the Slide Show tab.

2. In the Monitors group, click the down arrow in the Resolution field.

3. Select 640×480 (Fastest, Lowest Fidelity).

This option speeds up the performance while lowering the fidelity of the presentation. You will need to run the slide show in its entirety to see how clarity is affected. If the change is too dramatic, you can select the Use Current Resolution option or try the other options: the 1024×768 (Slowest, Highest Fidelity), which offers a crisp image but slows down the performance, or the 800×600 option, which is the "middle ground" between the two other options.

As a reminder, if you're sending the presentation via email, be sure to zip or compress it before sending to ensure it goes through as fast as possible.

In this chapter, you learned about when to consider movies as an option in your presentation, along with compatible file formats and conversion options. You also learned how to insert a movie or animated GIF into your presentation. You also saw two examples of using animated clip art with a movie or a picture as a background to the movie. In the next chapter, you'll learn about the many ways to use sound to enhance your presentation even more.

Adding Sound to Your Presentation

Like movies, sound can also add some life to your presentation. Whether you're trying to establish a mood, offer a narration, or simply drive home an important point, sound can give some sizzle to the steak. In this chapter, you'll learn how to insert sound files, how to start and stop the sounds, and how to set up objects and text to trigger the sounds. You'll also learn how to add CDs and record a narration.

When Sound Is Appropriate

Sound is wonderful when you're using it to help you make a point. But how many websites have you clicked on only to be greeted with blaring sound because you forgot to turn down the volume? Startling, isn't it?

That's why being prudent with sound is your best bet. If you're unveiling something new and different, a drum roll is appropriate. If you've achieved a significant company goal or objective, a little applause is in order. Or if you want some soothing background music during your presentation, sound can do the trick in helping communicate your message.

The bottom line is to use sound for specific reasons that enhance your presentation and make your messages memorable.

Supported Sound File Formats

PowerPoint 2007 supports the following sound file formats:

- **AIFF audio file**   Audio Interchange File Format (.aiff)

- **AU audio file**   Unix Audio (.au)

- **MIDI file**   Musical Instrument Digital Interface (.mid or .midi)

- **MP3 audio file**   MPEG Audio Layer 3 (.mp3)

- **Windows audio file**   Wave Form (.wav)

- **Windows Media audio file**   Windows Media Audio (.wma)

If your sound file is not in one of these formats, it will not play in Power-Point 2007. However, you can convert it to one of these formats using a utility, program, or add-in such as:

- Microsoft Windows Media Encoder, a free program that makes some files compatible with PowerPoint 2007. Visit http://www.microsoft .com/windows/windowsmedia/forpros/encoder/default.mspx for more information.

- PFCMedia, an add-in that automates the formatting of multimedia. For more information, visit PFCMedia for PowerPoint at http://office .microsoft.com/en-us/marketplace/EM012132961033.aspx.

When using sound files, you should note the difference between embedded and linked files, especially if you need to make changes. *Embedded* files are stored in the presentation file, whereas *linked* files are stored in their own files outside the presentation file. Here is information to help you determine when to use an embedded file or a linked file. You can use the Package For CD option to make it easier: Click the Microsoft Office icon and then Publish | Package For CD. You can copy the file to a folder or to a CD. The linked files are included as the default setting.

Embedded Sound Files	Linked Sound Files
Stored as part of the presentation.	Stored outside of the presentation file. Should be stored in the same folder as the presentation.
Must be deleted, edited in original file format, and reinserted for changes to appear in the presentation.	Changes appear in the presentation when you make a change to the source file.
If .wav files are less than 100KB (KB), you can embed them.	If .wav files are greater than 100KB or sound files are of any other media type, you must link them to, not embed them in, the presentation.

Inserting Sound Files

Adding sound to a PowerPoint 2007 file is similar to adding a movie, which you learned how to do in Chapter 10. You have four options for inserting sound files.

- **Sound From File**   This option lets you insert a sound clip or music file.
- **Sound From Clip Organizer**   You can choose from sounds like applause or light piano or holiday music.
- **Play CD Audio Track**   You select the CD track you want to play during the presentation.
- **Record Sound**   This option allows you to record your own sound for your presentation.

For now, we'll insert the sound file from the Clip Organizer.

1.   Go to the Insert tab.

2.   In the Media Clip group, click Sound.

3.   Click Sound From Clip Organizer.

4.   Select the sound you want to insert into the presentation. A sound icon will appear on the slide.

When you insert the sound, a Microsoft Office PowerPoint dialog box (shown next) asks when you would like to have the sound play. Your options are

- **Automatically**   Your sound will play when the slide appears.
- **When clicked**   When you click the sound icon, your sound will play. This is also known as a *trigger*.

MEMO

Be sure the sound file is long enough to play across the number of slides you need. You'll find the sound time in the Play Sound dialog box on the Sound Settings tab in the Information section. If you'd like to repeat the sound, check the Loop Until Stopped checkbox in the Sound Options group on the Sound Tools Options tab. The sound will continue playing until you stop it. You may find it easier to add sound after your presentation is completed, that way you'll know when you want to add, remove, or loop the sound.

PowerPoint offers another option on the Sound Tools Options tab. Go to the Sound Options group and select Play Sound and then Play Across Slides. This option plays the sound in its entirety one time. (If you'd like to play the sound continuously, check the Loop Until Stopped checkbox in the Sound Options group.)

If you choose the Play Across Slides option, you'll need to define the number of slides the sound should play across. Chapter 12 will cover animations in depth, but to establish the number of slides the sound needs to play across, follow these steps:

1. Go to the Animations tab.

2. In the Animations group, select Custom Animation.

3. From the Custom Animation Pane, select the line with the triangle.

4. Click the down arrow and then Effect Options.

5. In the Play Sound dialog box, go to the Effect tab.

6. In the Stop Playing section, select After and enter the number of slides the sound should play across.

Selecting How Sounds Should Start and Stop

The default setting for sound in PowerPoint 2007 is for the sound to play once in its entirety, but you can adjust the start and stop options for your presentation. To change the way the sound begins after you've inserted your sound file on the slide:

1. Click the sound icon.

2. Go to the Animations tab.

3. Select Custom Animation in the Animations group.

4. In the Custom Animation Pane, in the Modify: Play section, click the down arrow for the Start field.

5. Choose the way you want the sound to start: On Click, With Previous, or After Previous Slide.

Stopping and Starting Sound from One Location

What about starting and stopping sound from one location? You can adjust the way your narration starts and stops in the Play Sound dialog box. Click the sound icon on your slide. Select the Animations tab, and in the Animations group, select Custom Animation. From the Custom Animation Pane, select the line with the triangle. Click the down arrow and then select Effect Options. When the Play Sound dialog box appears, go to the Effect tab and from the Start Playing section, shown next, you can select:

- **From Beginning**   To start the sound file immediately

- **From Last Position**   To start the sound file from the last CD track played

- **From Time**   To begin the sound after establishing a time delay

For this example, click From Time and enter the number of seconds you'd like to delay the sound before playing.

In the Stop Playing section of the Play Sound dialog box, you can stop playing the sound. The options are: On Click, the default setting, which stops the sound when you click the mouse; After Current Slide; or After. You can use the After option to play across a selected number of slides, as you learned in the previous section of this chapter. Select this option and enter the number of slides for the sound to play across.

Setting Up Slide Elements to Trigger Sounds

Adding text or objects with sound is easy in PowerPoint 2007. Let's look at ways to add a sound to bulleted text:

1. Add the bulleted text to your slide.

2. Highlight the bullets you want to add animation and sound to.

3. Go to the Animations tab.

4. In the Animations group, click the down arrow next to the Animate field.

5. Select the way you want your bullets to appear on the slide. (You'll learn more about animations in Chapter 12.)

6. Click Custom Animations in the Animations group.

7. Click the down arrow to the right of the bullet.

8. Select Effect Options.

155

9. In the Enhancements section on the Effect tab, click the down arrow next to the Sound field.

10. Select the sound you want to add.

This will add the same sound to all the bullets. If you want to add a different sound to each bullet, click the doubled down arrow (circled below) to the left under the first bullet of text to display all the bullets.

Now that you can see all the bullets, click the down arrow to the right of the bullet you want to add sound to. Then select Effect Options, and in the Enhancements section on the Effect tab, click the down arrow next to the Sound field. Select the sound you want to add to this bullet. Continue doing this with each bullet you'd like to change the sound on.

Playing CDs with Slide Shows

Sometimes you may want to play a certain song during your presentation. You can easily use music from a CD while giving your presentation. Just remember the CD is still separate from your presentation; it is not linked to or embedded in the presentation file.

1. Insert the CD into your computer's CD drive.

2. Select the slide that you want the music to begin playing on.

3. Go to the Insert tab.

4. In the Media Clips group, select Play CD Audio Track.

5. In the Insert CD Audio dialog box, enter the Start At track number and the End At track number.

6. Change the times in the time boxes as needed.

7. Click OK.

8. Select when you would like the CD to play: Automatically or When Clicked.

MEMO

Voice narration overrides other sounds, with only one sound playing at a time. If you have other sounds set to play automatically, they will not play if a narration is included. If you have set the sounds to play When Clicked, however, they will continue to play when you click them in the order you established.

Recording a Narration with Slide Shows

The ability to record a narration with your PowerPoint 2007 presentation is the perfect answer for those times when more information is needed for a fuller presentation. You can record a narration before or during a presentation, and you have the option of recording narration for one slide or for the entire presentation.

To record the narration, you'll need a sound card, microphone, and speakers on your computer. These options have become standard on most recently built computers and generally offer enough sound quality for your narration needs. If you want to enhance the sound, however, you can look into upgrading your sound card and/or purchasing a USB microphone that plugs directly into your computer's USB port.

To record your narration, follow these steps:

1. Click the slide you want to begin the recording on.

2. Go to the Set Up group on the Slide Show tab.

3. Click Record Narration.

4. In the Record Narration dialog box (shown below), click Set Microphone Level.

5. Read the text in the Microphone Check dialog box to test your volume and make sure your microphone is working.

6. Click OK to begin recording.

MEMO

To make sure you don't lose any of the narration at the beginning or end of recording, wait a moment or two before moving on to the next slide. If you move too quickly, the recording may cut off too soon.

When you click OK before you start recording, you'll embed the narration into the presentation. If you'd prefer to link to the narration file, go to the Record Narration dialog box and check the Link

Narrations In checkbox. Then click the Browse button and select the folder where you want to store the narration file. Remember to save your narrations and presentation in the same folder.

PowerPoint 2007 automatically records the time spent on each slide. You can save these timings with the narration when the dialog box appears at the end of your recording. This works well when you want the narration to run automatically with your presentation. You can also choose to set the timings manually or turn them off completely. (Note, however, that this does not delete the timings; it simply turns them off until you turn them back on again.)

To set the timings manually, go to the Animations tab and the Transition To This Slide group. In the Advance Slide section, check the Automatically After checkbox. Enter the number of seconds you'd like for the slide to stay on the screen.

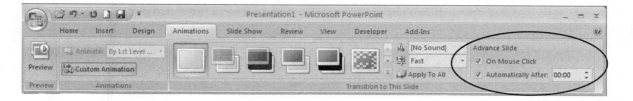

To turn off the timings, go to the Slide Show tab and click Set Up Slide Show to access the Set Up Show dialog box. In the Advance Slides section, select Manually. To turn the timings back on from the Set Up Show dialog box (shown next), in the Advance Slides section, select Using Timings, If Present.

If you want to record a narration during a presentation, follow the same steps described previously. If you need to pause your narration, right-click the slide, and from the shortcut menu, select Pause. To resume narration, right-click the slide, and from the shortcut menu, select Resume.

Occasionally, you may want to record comments during a presentation.

1. In the Normal view of the presentation, select the slide that you'll add the comment to.

2. Go to the Insert tab.

3. In the Media Clips group, click Sound.

4. Select Record Sound.

5. In the Record Sound dialog box, click Record and record your comment.

6. When you're finished, click Stop.

7. Type in the name of the comment and then click OK.

The sound icon will appear on the slide.

In this chapter, you learned when to consider adding sound to your presentation, how to insert and adjust sound files, how to set up text and objects to trigger the sound, and how to use CDs and narrations to enhance your presentation. We briefly touched on animations in this chapter, but in the next chapter, you'll learn about animations in more detail.

HOW DOES YOUR VOICE SOUND?

When you're recording a narration, be aware of how your voice sounds. For example, if you're reading directly from a script, rehearse it a few times so you sound more natural instead of like you're reading.

Do you have a tendency to sound monotone? Then look closely at what you're reading or saying and find spots where you can offer a bit of inflection to make it more interesting for the listener. The rise and fall of your voice can make the difference in whether you excite or bore the listener.

Are you enunciating? Wake up that lazy tongue so it doesn't lie in the back of your throat or say hello-o-o-o to lips that don't open fully. Practice over-enunciating this phrase a few times to get your mouth warmed up: "The lips, the teeth, and the tip of the tongue." Over-enunciating may seem strange when you

rehearse, but once you begin recording, you'll fall into an easy and understandable rhythm that sounds natural.

Does your voice have a tendency to go into the upper regions that only dogs can hear? Then practice keeping your voice in the lower ranges and record yourself as you practice. This way, you'll know what sounds pleasing to the ear.

No matter what your voice issue is, you can improve it with some concentrated practice and by recording yourself regularly. If you're serious about making a change, hire a vocal coach who specializes in the spoken word. Or check your local college or university; many times, an abbreviated class may be open to non-students during the semester.

Creating and Using Animations

Part of the fun of using graphics in a presentation is the ability to animate them to increase their visual impact. Almost any object, including text, single bullets, and list items, can be animated. Plus, you can apply animation effects to individual slides, the Slide Master, or custom layouts.

With animation, you essentially bring a still object to life by allowing it to move on the slide. This movement is what captures the audience's attention. The trick to effective animation, however, is to use restraint. Too much animation can become overwhelming for viewers, in which case they can't focus on the information you want them to retain.

In this chapter, we'll take a look at how animation can be used effectively in a presentation. We'll also show you how to use built-in animations, create custom animations, and how to work with special animation effects. As a bonus in this chapter, we'll also explain how to rehearse a presentation and use Presenter View. You'll need these skills to be certain your animations are coming across as effectively as you think they are.

Overview of Animations

When you work with animations, keep in mind the design principles mentioned in Chapter 1. Simplicity, really, is the key to using animations successfully. Usually, a single animation is plenty for a given slide. Sometimes, however, multiple animations might be not only useful but also downright necessary.

For example, bulleted lists can sometimes be overpowering on a slide. Easing viewers into a concept slowly by displaying bullets one at a time might be more helpful. In this case, the use of multiple animations is the right choice: You can select an animation sequence that displays bullets only as you click the mouse. This method keeps the pertinent point on the screen and allows you to control when the audience sees the next pertinent point. Audience members who might be tempted to read ahead without listening to you are thwarted, and you remain in control of how—and when—your content is displayed.

On the other hand, if you use this approach but also apply busy animations to each bullet as it appears (for instance, each bullet flies in from the side or top of the slide, spinning as it drops into place), you might defeat the entire purpose of thoughtfully drawing your viewers through salient points one by one. Instead, their focus will be on wondering where the next bullet will come flying in from.

Animation speed is also an important consideration. Animate too many objects too quickly on a slide, and your audience might get dizzy. Animate objects too slowly, and your audience might nod off to sleep.

In the end, rehearsing your slide show is critical so you can see what your audience will see. Look at your presentation from their perspective, and you just might discover that a fun, quirky animation isn't really that cool after all.

Rehearsing Your Presentation

Before we get started with animations, let's take a minute to get up to speed on rehearsing slide shows. Rehearsing is a way to preview your presentation

that helps you catch any errors that might be visible to
viewers when the slide show runs. By rehearsing, you can
review animation timings, slide transitions, and special
effects. Knowing how to rehearse your presentation *before*
you add animations is helpful because you can then check
animations more effectively as you add them.

To perform a quick review of your presentation and
how your graphics look and act, you'll need to open your
presentation in Slide Show mode. To do that, open the
presentation and go to the Slide Show tab. In the Start Slide Show command
group, click From Beginning, as shown in Figure 12-1.

Click the mouse as needed to move slides along or watch as the slides play
automatically. The slide show will play using the method you set up. Note any
slides where graphics are incorrect or animations appear differently than you
anticipated. When the slide show finishes, click the screen to exit back into
Design mode.

Make any corrections needed to your graphics or animations, and then
replay the slide show to be certain you've fixed any problems. You might need
to repeat this process a few times, but the time spent is worth it if you can
catch and fix mistakes before an audience sees the presentation.

Rehearse Presentation Timing

Once you've confirmed that your graphics are behaving as they should, it's
a good idea to rehearse your presentation delivery. Rehearsing helps you get
comfortable with the show and lets you verify your show's timing is correct.
To rehearse a slide show, follow these steps:

1. Go to the Slide Show tab.

2. In the Set Up command group,
    click Rehearse Timings.

THE EASY WAY

You can also start
your slide show
by clicking From
Current Slide to
start the show
from the slide
you are currently
viewing within the
presentation.

165

3. Use the Rehearsal toolbar to advance to the next slide, pause, and repeat the slide as necessary. The toolbar also shows timings for individual slides as well as the overall presentation.

4. If you want to keep the recorded slide timings, click Yes in the message box that appears after the last slide timing is set. If you do not, click No.

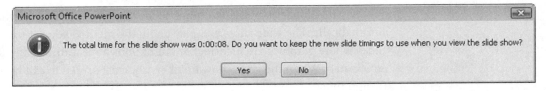

166

5. If you keep the slide timings, the presentation will switch to Slide Sorter View to show the presentation and the time it takes to play each slide.

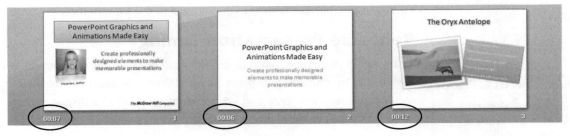

The rehearsed timings will automatically advance the slides for you the next time you play the slide show. Be careful here, however. Preset timings can advance slides before you're ready. This can cause your presentation to seem out of control in front of an audience. If you want to remove rehearsed slide timings temporarily, go to the Slide Show tab and clear the Use Rehearsed Timings checkbox in the Set Up group.

To begin using rehearsed timings again, simply go back and select the Use Rehearsed Timings checkbox. If you would rather set the timings for your slides manually instead of using the timings provided during rehearsal, follow these steps:

1.   Click the slide you want to set the timing for.

2.   Go to the Animations tab.

3.   In the Transition To This Slide command group, under Advance Slide, click to insert a check mark to the left of the Automatically After box.

4.   In the Timing box, use the up and down arrows to enter the number of seconds you want the slide to play.

167

INTRODUCING PRESENTER VIEW

One of the most helpful features in PowerPoint 2007 is Presenter View. This feature allows you to use two monitors as you present a slide show: One monitor displays the presentation as a slide show; the other monitor displays the slides along with other items that the audience never sees.

For example, speaker notes are displayed on the second monitor so you can easily refer to them while presenting. You can also select slides out of sequence, preview slide text so you know exactly what's going to happen when you next click the mouse, use your mouse as a pen to draw the audience's attention to items on a slide, and black out screen content as desired.

To enable this feature, you need to have a computer with multiple monitor capability turned on or a laptop that has dual display features. Then, to turn on multiple-monitor support in PowerPoint 2007, go to the Slide Show and in the Monitors command group, select Use Presenter View. Then click the arrow next to Show Presentation On and select a monitor.

Once the monitors are set up, go to the Slide Show tab and in the Set Up command group, select Set Up Slide Show. Select the options you want to use during the presentation (such as pen colors) and click OK.

When you're ready to present, go to the View tab and in the Presentation Views command group, select Slide Show.

Using Built-In Animation Tools

Now let's move on to the real meat of this chapter: animations. When you work with animations, you'll be using two key areas of PowerPoint: the Animations tab and the Custom Animation pane. Figure 12-2 shows the Animations tab and its command groups: Preview, Animations, and Transition To This Slide.

Figure 12-2 The Animations tab

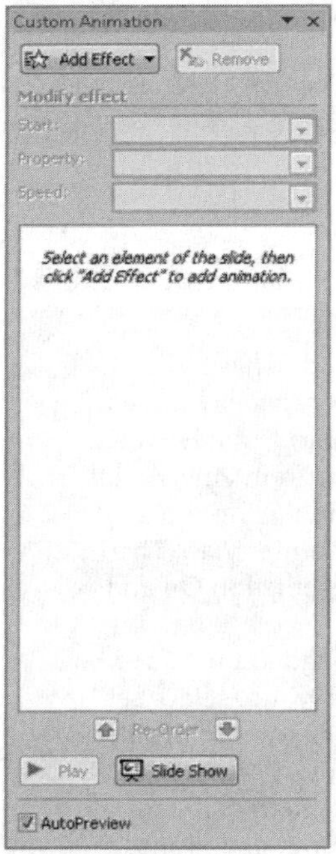

Figure 12-3 shows the Custom Animation pane, which is opened by clicking Custom Animation in the Animations command group on the Animations tab.

When you use the Animations tab, you can quickly access built-in animations. These are three very basic animations that can be applied with a single click: Fade, Wipe, or Fly In. You can also easily specify how quickly those animations occur. The Custom Animation pane, on the other hand, provides a much more detailed list of animation options. We'll explore the Animations tab options first, and then we'll take a look at the possibilities available with the Custom Animation pane.

Applying Animations from the Animations Tab

If you're simply looking for a quick way to animate an object, use the Animations command group on the Animations tab. The Animate command offers three commonly used animation selections available through the drop-down menu:

- **Fade** The object will move from invisible to visible. This animation is actually the *opposite* of fading, which implies an object will become paler.

Figure 12-3 The Custom Animation pane

- **Wipe**   The object will appear as if someone were wiping it onto the slide.

- **Fly In**   The object will fly in from the bottom of the slide.

Click the animation you prefer. You can click Preview in the Preview command group to see how the animation will look.

PowerPoint will apply a default speed of Fast to these animations. To change the default, go to the Transition To This Slide command group and change the speed from Fast to Slow or Medium.

Applying Animations from the Custom Animation Pane

If you're looking to do more with your animations than the few simple options provided on the Animations tab, you'll need to use the Custom Animation pane. This pane lets you control how items appear on the slide and the way multiple effects impact one another. The options vary depending on the animation applied to a given object, but they include:

- **Add Effect**   Includes Entrance, Emphasis, Exit, and Motion Path options. Each option then offers a menu of animation choices to select from.

- **Remove**   Lets you remove the animation applied to an object.

- **Start**   Offers the choice of whether to start an animation on a mouse click, with a previous object, or a certain amount of time after a previous object appears on the slide.

- **Path**   Offers the option to lock or unlock a path, edit points on a path, or reverse the path direction.

- **Speed**   Offers animation speed options from Very Slow to Very Fast.

- **Size**   Lets you select the size and direction an object grows.

- **Play**   Lets you play the animation on demand.

- **Slide Show**   Starts the slide show from the current slide.

- **AutoPreview**   Shows you the animation.

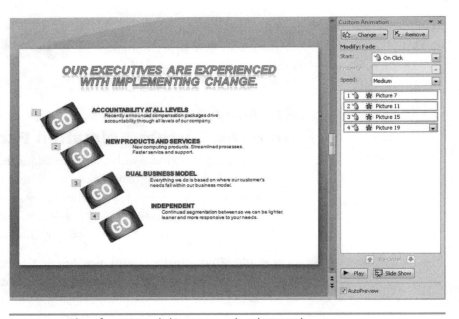

Figure 12-4   These four animated objects are numbered separately.

We'll outline specific steps for you next, but first we want you to see the Custom Animation pane at work. Here's an example of how using the Custom Animation pane can make a big difference: In Figure 12-4, the four GO graphics are set up as four separate animated objects. They are each set to fade separately into the document on individual mouse clicks. In Figure 12-5, however, those four separately animated objects have been grouped together

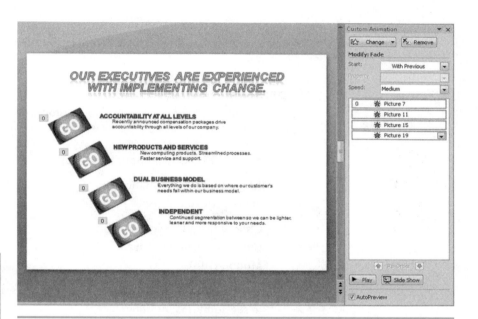

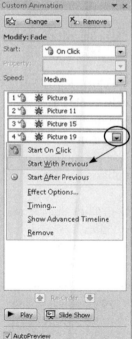

Figure 12-5   These four separate objects are animated as a single object and all appear with a single number, 0 in this case, on the slide itself. In the Custom Animation pane, they appear with the 0 next to the first object in the group, and the remaining items fall under without any number to indicate they belong with the first object.

so they all fade onto the slide as a single, cohesive group. In addition, they have been set up to fade in automatically—just one mouse click is required.

The difference is in how the animations were set up in the Custom Animation pane. In Figure 12-4, each object is numbered separately 1 through 4. In Figure 12-5, each object is numbered 0. We accomplished this by animating each object separately, and then selecting all the objects in the Custom Animation pane, and using the menu command Start With Previous. You can't create these kinds of advanced animations using the simple commands on the Animations tab; you need to become skilled at using the Custom Animation pane if you want to truly take advantage of the animation features in PowerPoint 2007.

Go ahead and open the Custom Animation pane now (Animations | Custom Animation). You'll need to have it open for the next several sections in this chapter.

Separately Animate Objects

To animate objects separately using the Custom Animation pane, follow these steps:

1. Select the object you want to animate.

2. In the Custom Animation pane, click Add Effect.

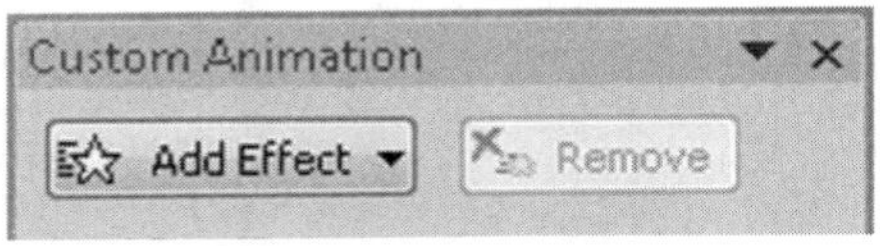

3. Choose the effect you want (Entrance, Exit, Emphasis, Motion Path).

4. Use the mini-menus to select the effect you want or click More Effects to see additional options.

That's it—each item is now separately animated. In the Custom Animation pane, each animated object should be numbered separately. Beside each object number you'll see icons and identification information for the object. For example, in Figure 12-6, each object is shown with a mouse icon to indicate the animation will occur on a mouse click; a symbol beside the mouse icon shows whether the animation is an entrance, exit, or emphasis animation; and every object is identified as a different picture.

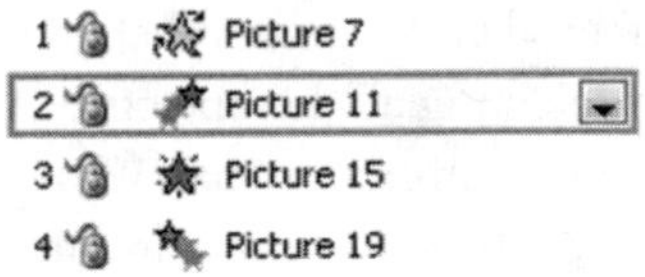

Figure 12-6   The Custom Animation pane will clearly show you which animations have been applied to each object and when those animations are scheduled to occur.

Also notice the down arrow in Figure 12-6. Click this arrow, and you'll see the shortcut menu shown in Figure 12-7.

This shortcut menu lets you change the effects and scheduled timing of the animation. Click Effect Options or Timing and a dialog box will appear. The dialog box will be named according to the animation you've selected; you can select the Effect and/or Timing tabs and make the changes appropriate for animation in question.

Figure 12-7   Each animated object can be modified quickly using the shortcut menu.

For example, an object that has been animated with the Appear effect will display sound and dimming options whereas an object that has been animated with the Diamond effect will display direction and sound options instead. You'll need to take a close look at each object's Effect tab to determine which options are available.

The Timing tab will typically show standard timing options for every effect, though:

- **Start**   Start the animation on a mouse click, with a previous animation, or a certain amount of time after the last animation.

- **Delay**   Tell PowerPoint to delay the animation for a certain amount of time after the Start option selected.

- **Speed**   Select from Very Slow to Very Fast. A bonus to using the tab is that it displays the exact time in seconds, which PowerPoint doesn't provide when you set the speed from the Animations tab or at the top of the Custom Animation pane.

- **Repeat**   Repeat the animation according to your preferences.

- **Rewind When Done Playing**   Use this option for movies; you can tell PowerPoint to rewind the movie when it finishes playing.

- **Triggers**   Choose to trigger an animation as part of a click sequence or start the animation when a different object on the slide appears.

173

MEMO

A word of caution when linking objects to animate as a group: PowerPoint will do exactly what you tell it to do; so if you group objects and then move them up or down in the Custom Animation pane, you will find the objects displaying when you least expect them to. You've told PowerPoint to Start With Previous, remember, so as objects move, they then become linked to new "previous" items. Take your time and carefully lay out the slide *before* you attempt to group objects together. Watch for "invisible" objects, too—objects that are now hidden behind others as you worked on your slide. Hidden objects can make your animations work strangely, so if you're experiencing trouble take a close look for these issues in particular.

Combine Objects for a Single Animation

To animate multiple objects as a single object like we showed in the previous example shown in Figure 12-5, follow these steps:

1. Select each object you want to animate, and apply the animation effect you want to each one object individually.

2. In the Custom Animation pane, click the first object in the group you want to create. Press CTRL on your keyboard, and click to select the additional objects you want to include in the group.

3. Click the down arrow to open the shortcut menu; select Start With Previous.

The objects will now be linked together as a group.

Apply Animations to Bulleted Text

This animation is really easy to do and very effective with audiences because it keeps them from reading ahead as you present important points on a slide. Simply highlight the text in a bullet, and click Add Effect in the Custom Animation pane. Apply the effect you want, and select when you want the effect to start. Applying the same effect to all bullets in a group is best; switching effects can distract your audience.

Adding Animations to Tables

Animating parts of a table used to be pretty easy in PowerPoint, but PowerPoint 2007's increased table sizes makes it more difficult. You can't just ungroup and animate parts of a table like you could in previous versions. You can, however, still apply some effects to a table to make it appear as if parts of the table are animated. Essentially, you're going to change your table from an object to a picture file and then ungroup parts of it and animate the specific parts you want.

MEMO

At this point, you'll see a second version of the table on your slide. This second version is actually a picture of your table. Don't delete the original table until you've completed the entire process and are happy with the results. In fact, saving the original table on a slide at the back of your presentation just in case you need the original again is a great idea.

Animating a table is a pretty lengthy process; follow these steps slowly the first few times until you get the hang of them and you'll discover it's actually not that difficult to do.

1. Select the table and go to the Home tab.

2. Click Copy in the Clipboard command group.

3. Click the arrow under Paste in the Clipboard command group.

4. Click Paste Special.

5. Click Picture (Enhanced Metafile).

6. Click OK.

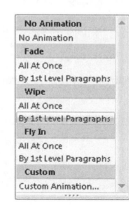

7. Double-check to be certain your table is placed exactly where you want it on the slide. If you try to move it later, you could run into trouble.

175

THE EASY WAY

There is another way to animate bulleted text, however. Click the text box, and then go to the Animations tab. In the Animations command group next to Animate, select All At Once or By 1st Level Paragraphs under Fade, Wipe, or Fly In. Using this method ties together all the bulleted text as a text group in the Custom Animation pane, which makes it easier to move that text around on the slide and maintain the bulleted animation effects. The only caveat here is that the text will automatically appear bullet by bullet after the first mouse click if you choose By 1st Level Paragraphs, so you might want to change the timing to coordinate your speaking with the bullets.

MEMO

Click outside the table to eliminate the number of groupings shown. Doing this will give you a better view of the table so you can select the items you want to animate.

8. If the new picture is not selected, select it and go to the Picture Tools Format tab.

9. Click Group in the Arrange command group.

10. Click Ungroup.

11. Click Yes when prompted to convert the picture to a Microsoft Office drawing object.

12. Go to the Drawing Tools Format tab.

13. Click Group in the Arrange command group.

14. Click Ungroup.

15. Press CTRL and then click the portions of the table that you want to animate.

16. On the Drawing Tools Format tab, click Group in the Arrange command group.

17. Click Group.

18. Go to the Animations tab.

19. Click Custom Animation to open the Custom Animation pane.

20. In the Custom Animation pane, click Add Effect.

21. Select the effect you want to apply.

22. Add any other animation features you want using the Custom Animation pane.

MEMO

Do not try to regroup the entire table when you're done. Your animation effects will not apply if you do. This makes it difficult to move the table around on the slide, so be sure you've placed the table where you want it before you apply the steps in this process.

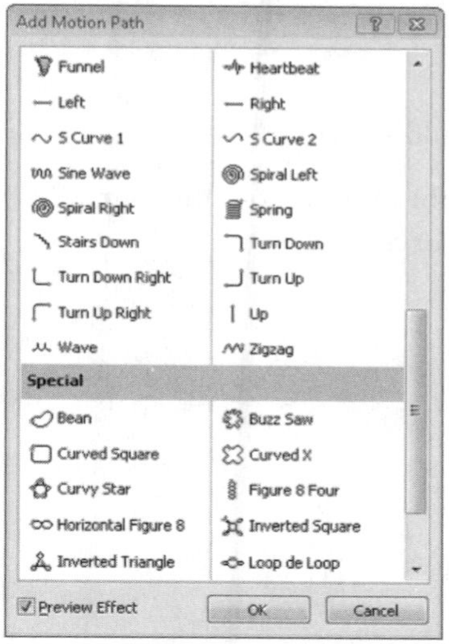

Creating Motion Paths

Motion paths can be a lot of fun to work with, and they are really quite simple to apply. A *motion path* is used when you want your object to do something beyond a traditional animation effect. You can create your own motion path, or you can apply one of more than 60 preset motion paths (see Figure 12-8).

To apply a preset motion path, follow these steps:

1. Click the object you want to animate.

2. In the Custom Animation pane, click Add Effect.

3. Select Motion Paths and click a path from the option shown.

4. If you want to see more options, click More Motion Paths, select a motion, and click OK.

Figure 12-8   PowerPoint 2007 offers more than 60 preset motion paths that you can apply to an object.

Once a motion path is applied to an object, the motion will be displayed next to the object on the slide when the Custom Animation pane is open, as shown in Figure 12-9.

Figure 12-9   Motion paths will be displayed next to the object.

To create your own custom motion path, follow these steps:

1. Click the object you want to animate.

2. In the Custom Animation pane, click Add Effect.

3. Select Motion Paths | Draw Custom Path. Choose from the four options shown (Line, Curve, Freeform, or Scribble).

4. Using your mouse, draw the path for the object.

MEMO

Use Transition Sound and Transition Speed options in the Transition To This Slide command group to add sounds to or change the speed of the transition.

Adding Animation Using Slide Transitions

Slide transitions help the audience move from one concept to another. Using the same transition effect throughout a presentation is a good idea, but if you're discussing different major concepts, you can effectively add a major slide transition to alert the audience to the change.

Transitions can be applied to individual slides or to all slides in a presentation. A Quick Styles Gallery makes it very easy to apply transitions, and this can be a simple way to add a little animation to a presentation without much work on your part.

To apply the same slide transition to every slide in a presentation, follow these steps:

1. Open the presentation in Normal View.

2. Go to the Slides tab in the left pane.

3. Click any slide thumbnail in the pane.

4. Go to the Animations tab.

5. In the Transition To This Slide command group, click a transition style from the Quick Styles Gallery. You can use the More arrow to see the entire gallery as shown to the left.

6. In the same group, click Apply To All.

If you prefer to add a different slide transition to each slide, simply click the slide thumbnail on the Slides tab of the left pane and follow these same steps *except* for Step 6. As you hover your mouse over various transition options, watch the slide to see a Live Preview of each transition.

In this chapter, you learned how to work with animations in a variety of ways, including built-in animations and custom effects. In the next chapter, we'll show you how to import Excel content into PowerPoint.

179

Importing Excel Content into PowerPoint 2007

PowerPoint 2007 makes it easy to use Excel content within your presentation. You can copy a chart or worksheet data from Excel to your presentation or simply create your own chart within PowerPoint. This will save you time and a lot of headaches because you enter the data only once and move it to the appropriate place.

Compatibility is not only a time-saver but also a quick way to make your presentations look sharper and more professional. Let's take a look at how you can move information to PowerPoint with just a few mouse clicks.

Sending a Chart from Excel to PowerPoint

If you want to copy a chart created in an Excel spreadsheet to PowerPoint, follow these steps:

1. Highlight the embedded chart or chart sheet in Excel.

2. On the Home tab, go to the Clipboard group.

3. Click Copy.

4. In PowerPoint 2007, select the presentation slide where you want to paste the chart.

5. Go to the Home tab and in the Clipboard group, click Paste.

6. Click the Paste Options icon next to the chart and select one of these options:

   - **Chart**   Pastes a chart linked to Excel data
   - **Excel Chart**   Includes the entire workbook
   - **Paste As A Picture**   Pastes the chart as a picture
   - **Keep Source Formatting**   Retains the chart's original formatting
   - **Use Destination Theme**   Pastes and formats the chart using the presentation's theme

The Paste Options icon disappears if you move or click away from the chart when you paste it.

MEMO
You also have other options for pasting the chart into your presentation. In PowerPoint 2007, go to the Home tab and from the Clipboard group, select Paste | Paste Special. From the Paste Special dialog box, you can paste the chart in a number of ways— as a graphic object, bitmap, or picture in a few different formats.

Copying Worksheet Data into PowerPoint

In PowerPoint 2007, you have a few different options for entering data. You can copy data from an Excel worksheet into PowerPoint, create an Excel spreadsheet in PowerPoint to enter your data into directly, paste data from other formats, or add hyperlinks.

1. In Excel, select the data you want to copy from the worksheet.

2. Go to the Home tab in the Clipboard group.

3. Click Copy.

4. In PowerPoint 2007, select the slide you want to paste the data into.

5. Go to the Home tab.

6. In the Clipboard group, select Paste.

7. Click the Paste Options icon next to the data on the slide and select one of the following:

   ■ **Keep Source Formatting**   Maintains the original format

   ■ **Use Destination Theme**   Uses the document theme applied to the PowerPoint presentation

   ■ **Keep Text Only**   Pastes the data as text

Select the Table Tools Design tab to add various formatting options such as color, borders, fill, and special effects. Chapter 6 describes how to use tables in PowerPoint 2007.

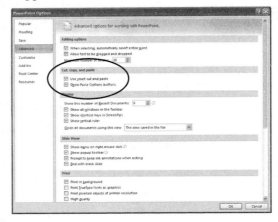

If you don't see the Paste Options icon, you may need to turn it on. Click the Microsoft Office button and then click PowerPoint Options, as shown below on the left. Select | Advanced | Cut, Copy, And Paste | Show Paste Options Buttons (shown on the right). If you paste data into a PowerPoint table, the Paste Options icon does not appear.

You can also create a functional Excel sheet directly in your presentation. Go to the Insert tab, and from the Tables group, select| Table | Excel Spreadsheet. A spreadsheet will appear on the slide for entering data, along with commands to perform Excel functions, as shown in Figure 13-1. Use the up and down arrows to move around in the spreadsheet when it is highlighted, or simply resize the spreadsheet by dragging the edges.

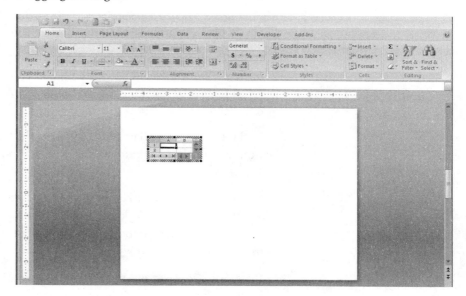

Figure 13-1   An Excel spreadsheet can be inserted directly in your presentation.

185

If you need to paste the data in another format such as a worksheet object, bitmap, or picture, go to the Home tab, and from the Clipboard group, select Paste | Paste Special. From the Paste Special dialog box, select the format you'd like to use.

Here are a few options for pasting into PowerPoint:

- If you need to edit the worksheet later, select Microsoft Office Excel Worksheet Object. This option lets you make changes to the entire worksheet along with changing confidential data that you don't want to display.

- If you want to paste the data using *Object Linking and Embedding (OLE)* and as a PowerPoint icon instead of including the actual content, select Microsoft Office Excel Worksheet Object and select the Display As Icon checkbox. In your presentation, click the icon to see the content.

- In the Paste Special dialog box, you can ensure the table in the presentation is updated when changes are made to the Excel data by selecting Paste Link. This will link to the source file and maintain the original formatting from Excel.

- In the Paste Special dialog box, you can select Attach Hyperlink if you want to include a hyperlink in the presentation to your source data in Excel.

- By clicking the down arrow in the Paste command group, you can select Paste As Hyperlink to insert a hyperlink to the source data in Excel. (Be sure to save the source data before attaching a hyperlink or this option will not work.)

- If you want to paste as a picture, you can select Device Independent Bitmap, Bitmap, Picture (Enhanced Metafile), or Picture (Windows Metafile).

- To paste as text, click Formatted Text (RTF) or Unformatted Text.

- You can also paste the data in the HTML format by selecting HTML Format.

- You can expand the range of data pasted into your presentation when the correlating data on the Excel worksheet expands. Just define a name for the range of Excel data before you copy it, and then you can paste a link to that range. From the Home tab, go to the Clipboard group and select Paste | Paste Special. In the Paste Special dialog box, click Paste Link and select Microsoft Office Excel Worksheet Object from the drop-down list. This option works when you copy data that isn't in table format in Excel.

Creating a Chart in PowerPoint

You can create a chart in PowerPoint by entering data directly into the presentation.

1. Go to the Insert tab.

2. In the Illustrations group, click Chart.

3. From the Insert Chart dialog box, select the type of chart you want to create.

4. Click OK.

In the Excel spreadsheet that appears, enter your data as shown in Figure 13-2. The changes will appear on the chart in your presentation.

In this chapter, you learned how simple it is to move Excel content to your PowerPoint presentation or to create your own Excel charts within PowerPoint. The next chapter covers moving graphics between Word and PowerPoint.

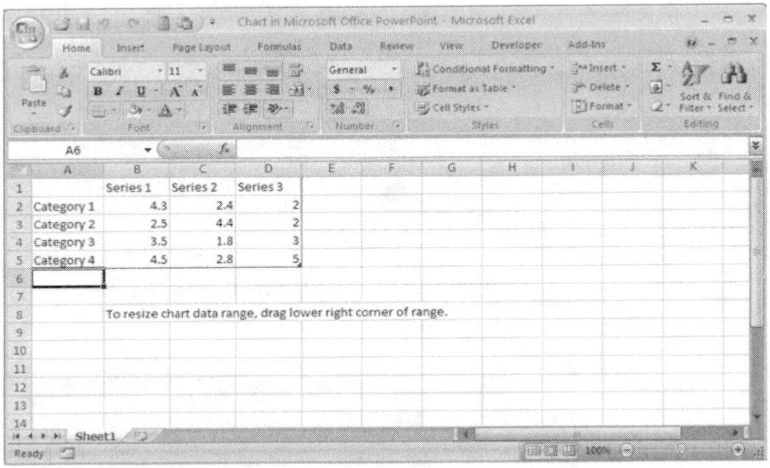

Figure 13-2 An example of the Excel spreadsheet where you can add data to create a chart in PowerPoint 2007

Moving Graphics Between Word and PowerPoint

One of the best things about PowerPoint 2007 is the ability to move items back and forth between applications. Sure, you still need to watch out for a few things, but for the most part, moving graphics between PowerPoint 2007 and Word is pretty straightforward. In this chapter, we'll look at how easy it is to move graphics between these applications; review the various ways you can format the object, text, or picture; and point out the exceptions to pasting in both applications. As a reminder, graphics can include clip art, pictures, charts, tables, or bulleted text.

Moving a Graphic from PowerPoint to Word

When you move a graphic from PowerPoint to Word, you have a few options, including resizing, that can help present the graphic accurately. From the Home tab in PowerPoint, go to the Clipboard group and select Copy (or press CTRL-C). In Word, select the place in the document where you want to paste the graphic and select Paste (or press CTRL-V).

When you paste into your Word document, you'll see the Paste Options icon appear, as shown in Figure 14-1. From here, you can choose from several options for inserting your graphic.

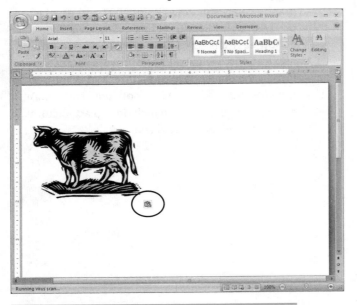

Figure 14-1   The Paste Options icon appears next to the graphic when moving a graphic from PowerPoint to Word.

Here's a rundown of what does and doesn't move easily from PowerPoint to Word:

- When moving pictures, shapes, SmartArt, and Clip Art to Word, you can select Paste As Picture, Keep Source Formatting, or Use Destination Theme.

- When moving a table to Word, you can select Paste As Picture, Keep Source Formatting, or Match Destination Theme.

- When moving a bulleted list to Word, you can select Paste As Picture, Keep Source Formatting, Match Destination Formatting, or Keep Text Only.

- When moving a chart to Word, you can select Chart, Excel Chart, Paste As Picture, Keep Source Formatting, and Use Destination Theme.

MEMO

Anytime you select the Paste As Picture option, you cannot make changes to the graphic you've inserted. So if you need to adjust any of your graphics, make the changes in PowerPoint before pasting the graphic into Word.

- When moving WordArt to Word, the only option that allows you to maintain the formatting is Paste As Picture. The other options—Keep Source Formatting, Match Destination Formatting, or Keep Text Only—will cause you to lose the WordArt formatting.

Let's review what some of these options mean.

- **Paste As Picture**   Pastes the graphic in as a picture

- **Keep Source Formatting**   Maintains the original format from PowerPoint

- **Use Destination Theme, Match Destination Theme, or Match Destination Formatting**   Inserts the graphic with the same document theme or format as the Word document

- **Keep Text Only**   Pastes as text into the Word document

- **Chart**   Pastes a chart linked to Excel data

- **Excel Chart**   Includes the entire workbook

Moving a Graphic from Word to PowerPoint

Moving a graphic from Word to PowerPoint is simple. From the Home tab in Word, go to the Clipboard group and select Copy (or press CTRL-C). In PowerPoint, select the slide where you want to paste the graphic and click Paste (or press CTRL-V). You'll see the Paste Options icon appear. Click to decide how to insert your graphic.

Sometimes, you'll find a font that you really want to use in your presentation or document. You can embed TrueType fonts in Word and PowerPoint to ensure you have the look you want. The steps are similar in both programs, but we'll look at how to do this in PowerPoint.

1. Click the Microsoft Office button.

2. Click PowerPoint Options.

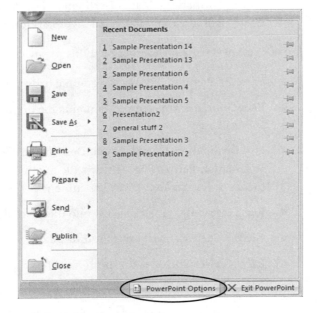

3. Select Save.

4. In the Preserve Fidelity When Sharing This Presentation section, select Embed Fonts In The File, as shown next.

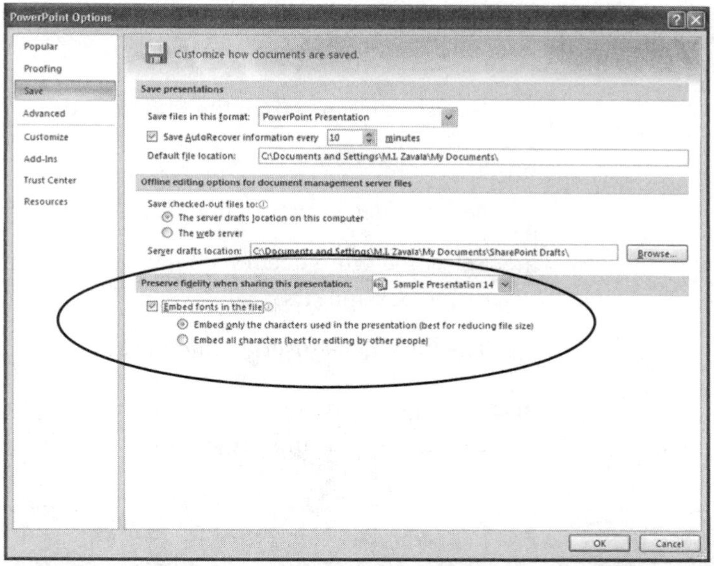

5. Click Embed Only The Characters Used In The Presentation checkbox.

6. Click OK.

Selecting Embed Only The Characters Used In The Presentation helps to reduce file size. Clicking Embed All Characters makes it easier if others are editing your presentation.

If you need to create a PowerPoint presentation based on an outline in a Word document, you can insert the outline directly in PowerPoint with a few mouse clicks. The Word file formats you can use are

- .doc (Microsoft Word 97–2003)

- .docx (Microsoft Word 2007)

- .txt (Text file)

- .rtf (Rich text format)

MEMO

If the Word document is in plain text and has no heading styles, PowerPoint will create an outline based on paragraphs created by hard returns when you press ENTER. For example, each item in a bulleted list is a paragraph and a title or subtitle is a paragraph.

You'll need to format the text in the presentation based on heading styles in the original Word document. In PowerPoint, follow these steps:

1. Go to the Home tab in the Slides group.

2. Click New Slide.

3. Select Slides From Outline.

4. Select the Word document you want to insert when the Insert Outline dialog box appears.

5. The file will be inserted into PowerPoint.

In this chapter, you learned how to move graphics back and forth between PowerPoint and Word, and you discovered different ways to format pictures,

FORMATTING AND THE BUILDING BLOCKS ORGANIZER

Although most graphics move easily from Word to PowerPoint, some lose their formatting when moved. One example of this is when you use Quick Parts on the Insert tab in Word. Quick Parts offers a Building Blocks Organizer for tasks you use regularly. Quick Parts has headers and footers, cover page designs, watermarks, text boxes, and more to help you put together a slick document. But although these building blocks work well in Word, they do not translate well to PowerPoint. You'll need to experiment to see which blocks you can use or adjust by copying and pasting them into a PowerPoint presentation. You can access Building Blocks Organizer in Word by going to the Insert tab, and from the Text group, select Quick Parts | Building Blocks Organizer. Insert the building block you want to include in your Word document.

THE EASY WAY

Distribute the document to other people

Package for CD
Copy the presentation and media links to a folder that can be burned to a CD.

Create Handouts in Microsoft Office Word
Open the presentation in Word and prepare custom handout pages.

Document Management Server
Share the presentation by saving it to a document management server.

Create Document Workspace
Create a new site for the presentation and keep the local copy synchronized.

Need handouts for your presentation in a hurry? PowerPoint 2007 offers you a quick way to create handouts so audience members can follow along with you, take notes, or simply have a source of information to refer to after the presentation. From your PowerPoint presentation, click the Microsoft Office button, and select Publish | Create Handouts In Microsoft Office Word. From the Send To Microsoft Office Word dialog box, select the layout you want or click Paste Link to link to the presentation. Paste Link will ensure that any updates to the PowerPoint 2007 presentation appear in the Word document. Click OK after you make a selection and print the handouts from your Word document. Remember to keep your presentation in the same folder as your Word document so the links work properly.

text, and objects effectively. You also learned about pasting exceptions that aren't as effective, and you got a quick tip for creating presentation handouts. In the next chapter, you'll learn about working with charts as design elements.

195

Working with Charts as Design Elements

Charts are a great way to share numerical information with an audience. Whereas SmartArt is a good choice for other types of information, charts are really your best bet when you have to explain numbers. They are a great way to illustrate and compare numerical data.

From the military to corporations around the world, charts are a universal method for sharing numerical data. Although we don't know when the chart was first invented, it's clear that once it was, the chart became a communication tool that could be used to bridge languages and cultures.

With PowerPoint 2007, adding a professional looking chart to a presentation is a pretty simple process; the Quick Style Galleries you've seen in other areas of PowerPoint are also available with charts, and three different Ribbon tabs allow you to make modifications to your charts quickly and easily.

In this chapter, we'll cover the commands available with each of the chart Ribbon tabs and show you how to create eye-catching charts.

A Quick Look at Charts

Charts in PowerPoint are linked automatically to Excel spreadsheets, so when you create a new chart you'll see an Excel spreadsheet open simultaneously on your screen. This nifty feature makes it easy to change or add chart data; you simply make the updates in the associated Excel spreadsheet and the information is applied to your PowerPoint chart automatically.

PowerPoint offers eleven different types of charts for you to choose from.

Chart	Description
Area	Places data into horizontal areas that show the relationship of each part to the whole
Bar	Uses horizontal bars to illustrate differences in individual pieces of data by using categories on the vertical axis and values on the horizontal axis
Bubble	Arranges data in a scattered format on a chart; compares sets of three values
Column	Uses vertical bars with categories organized along the horizontal axis and values along the vertical axis
Doughnut	Organizes data as a percentage of an entire pie and can contain more than one data series
Line	Plots data into lines and organizes categories on the horizontal axis and values along the vertical axis
Pie	Organizes data similarly to a doughnut chart but only contains one data series
Radar	Compares cumulative values of a number of data series
Stock	Arranges data in a specific order to illustrate fluctuations in stock prices and can also be used for scientific data
Surface	Shows the most favorable combinations between two sets of numeric data
XY	Similar to bubble charts but compares just two sets of data

MEMO

Creating a chart in Excel and importing it into PowerPoint is also a simple process. See Chapter 13 for more details.

To insert a chart, go to the Insert tab and click Chart in the Illustrations command group. Select the type of chart you want, and click OK. For illustration purposes, we chose the 3-D Area chart.

Once you've inserted the chart on your slide, a corresponding Excel spreadsheet will open. Although you can always use this spreadsheet to make changes to your data or chart information, go ahead and close it for now. We'll show you how to open it on demand in "Working with Data Commands."

Another thing you'll notice once a chart has been added to a slide is the addition of three new Ribbon tabs: The Chart Tools Design tab, the Chart Tools Layout tab, and the Chart Tools Format tab. In the following sections, we'll explore each.

The Chart Tools Design Tab

Click your chart to activate the new tabs, and then click the Chart Tools Design tab. It will look similar to the one shown in Figure 15-1, although specific chart styles and layouts will differ if you have chosen a different chart style than the one we're using.

From left to right, the Ribbon has four command groups: Type, Data, Chart Layouts, and Chart Styles.

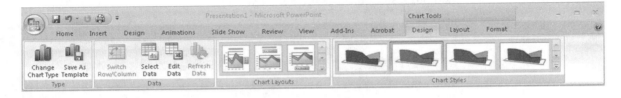

Figure 15-1 The Chart Tools Design tab

Using Type Options

You have two simple choices in the Type command group: You can change the type of chart, or you can save the current chart as a template. If you select Change Chart Type, you'll see the entire selection of available charts again. Just select a new one and click OK. The chart on your slide will automatically change.

If you want to save and reuse a particular type of chart, you can save it as a chart template. Add the chart to a slide, and then go to the Chart Tools Design tab and in the Type group, click Save As Template. Select the Charts folder, type in a name for your chart, and click Save.

Figure 15-2 Select Switch Rows/Columns to change the orientation of information on a chart.

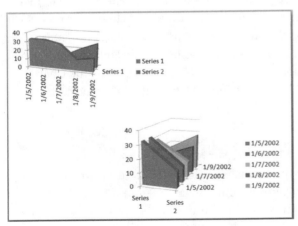

Working with Data Commands

When you need to change the data in your chart, you have a couple of different options available in the Data command group. Your chart might be easier for your audience to understand, for example, if row and column data are reversed. In that case, select the chart and select Switch Row/Column. Figure 15-2 shows how a simple change can make a chart look different. The top-left chart is the original version, whereas the bottom left shows the chart after using this command.

To change plotting order of a data series in a chart quickly, go to the Chart Tools Design tab, and from the Data group, click Select Data and highlight the data series and click Move Up or Move Down.

If you need to move the data to different locations in a chart, use the Select Data command. This opens the corresponding Excel spreadsheet, but it also opens the Select Data Source dialog box. This dialog box allows you to add, remove, move, and edit information or chart labels easily. You can also switch rows and columns using this dialog box.

If you prefer to just use the Excel spreadsheet to make changes, click Edit Data in this command group to open the spreadsheet. When data changes in a linked Excel spreadsheet or when the data otherwise needs updating, click Refresh Data to reflect the changes in your chart.

Changing a Chart Layout

If you decide that you still want to use the type of chart you've chosen, but you'd like a different layout, the Chart Layouts command group is the place to go. For example, we chose a 3-D Area chart type earlier in this chapter. Let's assume we still want an Area chart, but we no longer want it to be in 3D. In this case, we would choose a different chart layout by using the More arrow to open the Quick Style Gallery and select a new layout.

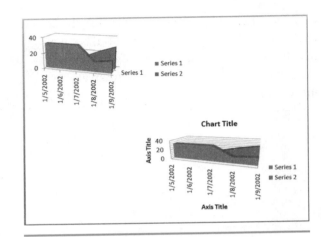

In Figure 15-3, the original 3D area chart is shown in the upper left whereas the new layout (Layout 6) is shown on the bottom right. The new layout provides chart and axis titles and substantially shortens the height of the chart itself.

Changing a Chart Style

If you're happy with the chart type and layout, but not so happy with the chart style, that's easy to change, too. Just click the More arrow in Chart Styles, and choose a new style from the gallery. You'll typically see multiple choices for every chart type, from multicolored versions to totally different colors that might contradict the theme you've applied to your presentation.

Figure 15-3   You can apply different layouts to the same type of chart.

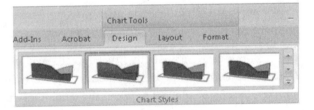

The Chart Tools Layout Tab

You can add a lot of details to your charts and work easily with chart elements using the Chart Tools Layout tab, as shown in Figure 15-4. There are six command groups on this tab: Current Selection, Insert, Labels, Axes, Background, and Analysis.

Using Current Selection

The Current Selection command group allows you to see which element of the chart is currently selected, and it gives you the ability to select and edit other elements instead.

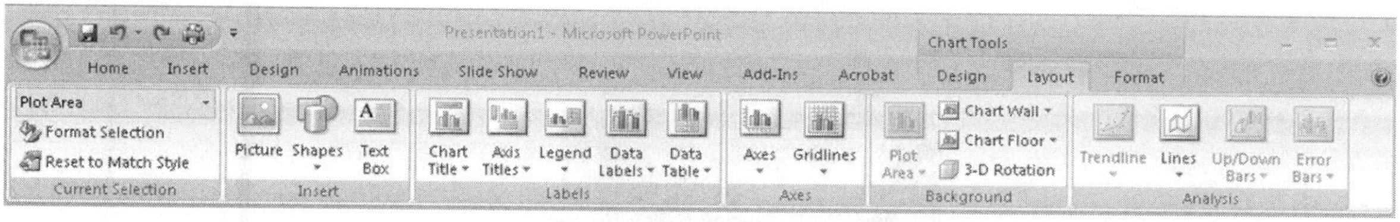

Figure 15-4   The Chart Tools Layout tab

At the top of the command group is a drop-down box with a down arrow beside it. Click the down arrow, and the entire group of elements used in the chart will be shown. To select an element, just highlight it. For example, in Figure 15-5, we've selected Plot Area.

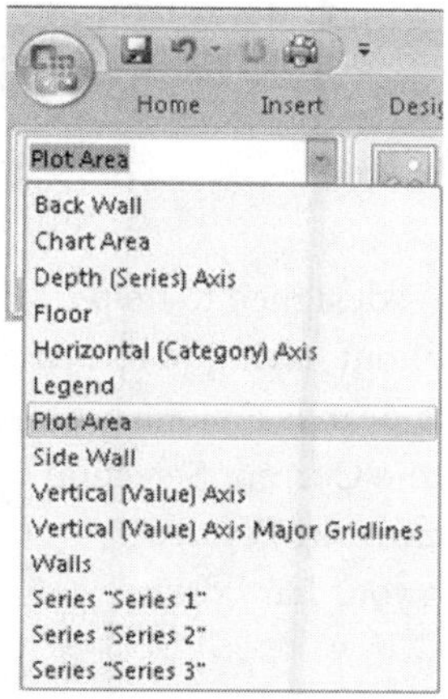

Once an element has been selected, you can format aspects of it by clicking Format Selection. The changeable aspects—such as Fill, Border Color, Shadow—will differ depending on the element you've chosen. Figure 15-6 shows the aspects available for the previously selected Plot Area element. Because the aspects have been covered in several other chapters throughout this book, we won't cover them here.

If you make changes and then decide you don't like them, you can start over again by clicking Reset To Match Style. This resets the chart to the original theme style of the presentation.

Figure 15-5   You can choose different chart elements to work with by using the menu in the Current Selection group of the Chart Tools Layout tab.

Figure 15-6   Each chart element has various aspects that you can change.

Using the Insert Command Group

The Insert command group doesn't work quite the way you think it will when you're working with charts. For example, if you try to select a chart element and then insert a picture into it, you'll be sorely disappointed because the picture simply won't drop into the chart element.

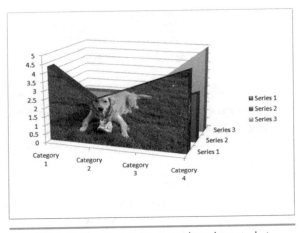

Figure 15-7   You can insert pictures in chart elements, but you'll need to use the Current Selection group instead of the Insert group.

This command group is really—as far as we can tell—designed to help you drop in pictures, shapes, and text onto the slide without having to return to the Insert tab. If you want to make a chart element appear as a picture, as in Figure 15-7, select the chart element and then go to the Current Selection command group and select Format Selection | Fill | Picture Or Texture Fill | Insert From File. Select the picture you want from your hard drive, and click Close.

Working with Labels

Some chart layouts will automatically provide you with a variety of chart labels, such as a title or a legend. Others won't. You can change or add chart labels using the Labels command group. Most label options typically allow you to select from an even larger menu to truly customize the label; look for the More *XX* Options selection at the bottom of each label menu.

- **Chart Title**   Lets you add a chart title without moving or resizing the chart (Centered Overlay Title) or simply add a title to the chart, resizing and moving the chart as necessary (Above Chart).

■ **Axis Titles**   Gives you different options, but essentially lets you add titles to the sides or bottom of your chart (shown on the right) and offers the option of stacking text or placing the titles horizontally.

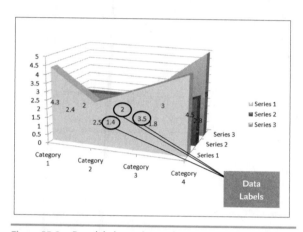

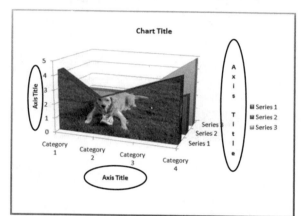

Figure 15-8   Data labels can be useful but use them sparingly to avoid overwhelming the audience.

■ **Legend**   Lets you display the chart legend in different areas.

■ **Data Labels**   Allows you to turn data labels on or off in your chart (see Figure 15-8).

■ **Data Table**   Shows the data in a table format near your chart. You can hide or show legend keys. If you show legend keys, be sure and remove them from any other area on the slide to avoid duplication.

Working with Axes

Sometimes you might not want to show axes information, or you want to modify how the axes information are displayed. In those cases, you'll find the Axes command group quite helpful. Click

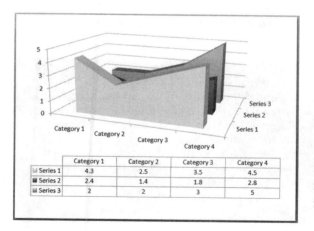

205

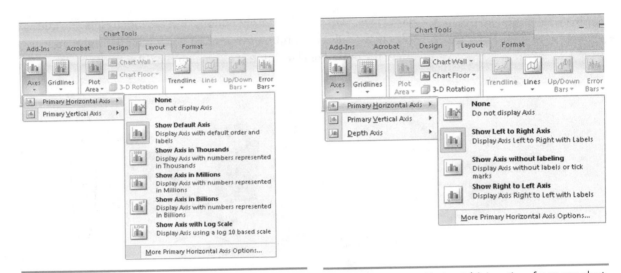

Figure 15-9 Primary Horizontal Axis options for a bubble chart   **Figure 15-10** Primary Horizontal Axis options for an area chart

Axes in the Axes command group, and you'll see a variety of horizontal and vertical axes options available, depending on the type of chart you've selected.

For example, if you're using a bubble chart, you might see Primary Horizontal Axis options like those shown in Figure 15-9. But if you're using an area chart, the options might look like those in Figure 15-10 instead. You'll need to do some exploration on your own to determine which options are

A WORD ABOUT GRIDLINES

You can eliminate, add, or modify gridlines in a chart by clicking the Gridlines command in the Axes group. Gridlines come in vertical, horizontal, or depth options. For audiences who are viewing the presentation in a large auditorium, try to stick with major gridlines as much as possible. Minor gridlines can be useful when you're dealing with important numbers that fall between major points on the chart's grid, but otherwise they can be distracting for an audience (see Figure 15-11).

Most charts will come with gridlines as a default; those gridlines are typically the best way to display the chart. However, don't be afraid to play around with gridlines a bit to see how they change the look and feel of your chart. In some cases, you just might find that adding a depth gridline or removing minor gridlines can be the touch you need to make your chart's information truly stand out.

Some charts, like a pie chart, won't even have axes so if you don't see some or all of the Axes commands available then your chart doesn't have a vertical or a horizontal axis.

Figure 15-11 Minor gridlines can clutter up a chart as shown in the top-left chart, but major gridlines (horizontal and vertical gridlines are both shown in bottom-left chart) can help an audience better understand a chart.

available for your charts. Simply click the option you want, and PowerPoint will apply it automatically to your chart.

Spicing Up the Background

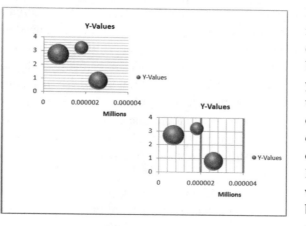

Many charts dropped into your presentation don't have much of a background to them. If you want to spice yours up a bit, you'll find the commands to help you out in the Background command group. Different chart types will have different background options available; if an option isn't available, then your chart doesn't use that particular option. And, depending on the theme used in your presentation, default options might be applied to your chart already.

Plot Area, for example, is used with bubble charts. Select Plot Area | Show Plot Area, and your chart will use a color automatically associated with your presentation theme. If you don't like that option, however, click More Plot Area Options and use a different color by adding the Fill option of your choice. Figure 15-12 shows the difference between a plot area that uses the presentation theme and one that uses a specially chosen fill color.

Chart Wall and Chart Floor options work in basically the same way; you're just changing the

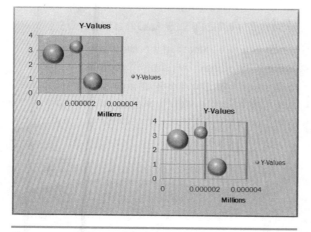

Figure 15-12 Because of the lines in the presentation theme, the lower-right chart's gridlines are more difficult to see. Adding a special fill color, as shown in the top-left chart, makes the gridlines easier to see, however.

vertical walls around the chart or the floor underneath it. You can either use the default selection provided by the presentation theme or apply your own colors.

The 3-D Rotation command, however, allows you to change the orientation of the information in a 3D chart. The command opens a dialog box that lets you adjust 3D presets that have been applied to the chart, the rotation of the axes, the perspective of the entire chart, the default position of the chart within its box, the depth of chart elements, and chart scale, as shown below.

Because every 3D chart can include so many different aspects, you'll need to work with each chart individually to determine which of the options to use in a given situation. The beauty of PowerPoint 2007 is that the dialog box makes it easy to play with the options; just use the up and down arrows for the different options, and watch as the chart changes in relation to your choices.

In Figure 15-13, you can see how simply changing Chart Scale Depth from 130 percent to 660 percent can make a stunning difference in the look of the same chart.

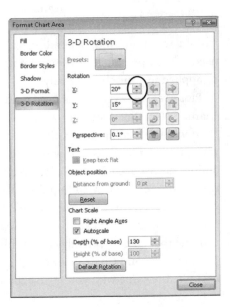

Using Analysis Commands

When you use a chart in a presentation, you're doing it (or should be doing it) to help the audience understand how numerical data impacts them. To help you with that, PowerPoint offers four analysis options that you can apply to charts:

■ **Trendlines**   Lines drawn on a chart that indicate the direction or trend of the data.

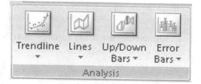

- **Lines**   *Drop lines,* which help clarify where data markers begin and end; *Series lines,* which emphasize the difference between data series; and *High-Low lines* that extend from the highest to lowest values in each chart category.

- **Up/Down Bars**   Lines that indicate the difference between data points in the first and last data series in a chart.

- **Error Bars**   Show potential error amounts related to data points or data markers. Error bars can be added to data series in 2D area, bar, column, line, xy (scatter), and bubble charts. For xy (scatter) and bubble charts, you can display error bars for the *x* values, the *y* values, or both.

MEMO

You can change the look and feel of these lines by clicking More *XX* Options at the bottom of a given menu to access the related dialog box. Simply make your selections from the dialog box.

To add or remove lines or bars, click the chart where you want to add or remove them, and then go to Chart Tools Layout tab, and from the Analysis command group, select the command you want to use. For example, we added a trendline to the chart in Figure 15-14 showing a downward trend in the data.

209

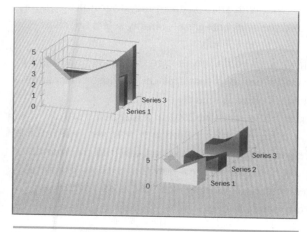

Figure 15-13   The same chart: Upper-left scale depth is 130 percent; lower-right scale depth is 660 percent.

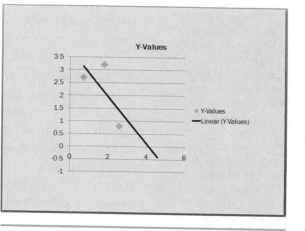

Figure 15-14   A trendline shows trends in data and can help viewers understand data easily.

The Chart Tools Format tab

The final tab available to you when working with charts is the Chart Tools Format tab, as shown in Figure 15-15.

Figure 15-15   The Chart Tools Format tab

For the most part, you've seen these different formatting options several times already in this book. Chapter 7 explains how to work with WordArt, and Chapter 8 explains the nuances of working with shapes. Except for the fact that it only applies to the chart you're working with, there's nothing really new on this tab.

So, if you want to make the title of a chart look cool by applying WordArt to it, this is the tab to use. Click the title text box, and apply the WordArt styles as desired. You do the same thing with shapes, grouping, ungrouping, sizing text boxes, slide gridlines, and the selection pane—simply select the chart element in question and use the tool on the tab.

If it were more difficult, we'd tell you! Even though this tab is redundant to other Ribbons in PowerPoint, its beauty is that it places all those commands right in front of you as you work on your chart.

And that truly is the beauty of PowerPoint 2007 in a nutshell, really. Everything you need is at your fingertips on a Ribbon tab. As you've learned throughout this book, once you're on the right tab, you can find commands quickly and easily. We hope you've learned a few new things about graphics and animations with PowerPoint 2007; looking like a pro is easy when you know the right tools and commands to use.

210

MEMO

Are larger 3D data markers blocking smaller ones in your chart? Select the chart element that needs to be moved, and then go to the Chart Tools Format tab, and from the Current Selection command group, select Depth Series Axis | Format Selection | Axis Options | Series In Reverse Order. Click Close.

Index

X

Y

Z